IS GOD PULLING THE STRINGS?

By

Rev. Dave Lakin

Foreword by Rev. John Partington

Former National Leader of Assemblies of God

In the UK and Ireland

CONTENTS

FOREWORD BY REV. JOHN PARTINGTON

I have known Dave for over 50 years so I am probably well qualified to write this short foreword for his autobiography. We have ministered together, been on holidays together, laughed and cried together and I know that his life story is one that will cause much blessing to a lot of people.

It is with that knowledge that I am happy to thoroughly endorse this book and trust that each reader will be both challenged and blessed by reading its contents.

Your lifelong friend,

John Partington

Is God pulling the strings?

CHAPTER 1

I DON'T LIKE SUNDAYS

It may surprise you, it may make you laugh, but Sundays used to be my least favourite day of the week. Every Sunday as a family, we would, after church, go to my grandma's house, but both my parents and grandma had some very strict rules regarding Sundays that had to be obeyed.

We were given the boys' comic books, the Eagle and Swift as we weren't allowed to watch any TV or play games. So after lunch we would sit in a chair and read our comics. Sunday was God's day, the Sabbath, so we had to 'rest' on Sundays. Behind my grandma's house was a local football pitch and we weren't even allowed to watch the game. However, we could see the pitch from one of the bedrooms, so I would go upstairs to watch the game. But if I heard the landing light go on or the door being opened to come upstairs, I would quickly run out of the bedroom, as I knew I'd be in trouble if caught out. So, Sunday was not a day that we looked forward to. We were always glad when

Sundays ended.

Sunday School was another reason why I did not like Sundays. I went to Sunday School because I had to. It was expected for me to go and I can tell you it was something that I never looked forward to! At Sunday School the teacher was more like a baby sitter, she was a member of the church, but there were no songs, no games, not even a Bible story! She would just drone on about boring things that none of us were particularly interested in. It was more like childcare to get the children out of the service. All I got to hear about in her lesson was how her football team had done the day before. But as she supported Barnsley F.C. I just wasn't interested!

One Sunday, which was more eventful than most, was when on the way to Sunday School the orchard I used to pass; was full of apples, pears and other fruits. I had plenty of time before I was about to be bored by stories of a rubbish football team that was the usual practice on a Sunday; so me and the twins Horace and Morris decided to jump over the wall and help ourselves. Back in the day this was known as scrumping, some of you older ones will know that already! What we didn't know at the time was that we'd been spotted. The next day the police arrived at my house to say that I might be taken to court for stealing. Fortunately, I didn't have to go to court but I never went back into the orchard. Horace and Morris landed in trouble too.

In terms of bodily constitution, I don't suppose it makes any difference where one is born, but I was glad to be born in South Yorkshire in a small town called Wombwell, the son of Irving a coal miner working at Houghton Main Colliery. That was in 1946 just after the Second World War had ended. I remember like it was yesterday my father coming home from the pit with a black face, a tired but happy man. He was proud to work hard for his family. My mother, Dorothy was a Godly woman, very caring, always looking out for those in need. Our house was always an 'open house', whoever came to visit were always made welcome.

My brother, Peter was two years older than me. Growing up together was good. We lived at number 35 Loxley Avenue, Wombwell – a small, terraced council house, with loads of lads of our own age living nearby. Naturally, Peter and I would have our moments when we would fight and fall out or argue; that would bring my mother into action! She had a bamboo cane that would come out and we would both receive our due punishment. Today, my mother would be in serious trouble with the authorities for doing that, but at the time, that kind of treatment seemed to stop us fighting and getting into too much trouble. The Bible has something to say on this matter – Proverbs ch. 13 v 24 says . . . Spare the rod, spoil the child.

Dorothy and Irving Lakin with Dave and Pete

School was not something I particularly excelled in and it became more apparent when my brother Peter had passed his 11 plus exam, which meant that he could go to a grammar school to continue his studies. He always was a bit cleverer than me! When he left school, he got a job as a Public Health Inspector. In those days grammar schools were the best schools to go to. When the 11 plus exams were being taken, I was in hospital having my tonsils out, so I missed the test, therefore my education was not to the same standard as my brother's. I attended the local comprehensive school, Wombwell High School. I left without any qualifications. This would be something that would on many occasions re-surface to stir up feelings of inadequacy and would really shake my self-confidence at points within my life. However, through God's promises, and at times miracles, I have overcome these instances where I have felt that my lack of education could hold me back. This book is a testimony of this!!

My Dad was a heavy smoker, he would smoke around 30 cigarettes a day, but the day he became a Christian, he came home from church, took every packet of cigarettes that he had, and threw them on the fire. From that day, until the day he died, he never smoked another cigarette. He was a very caring man; he looked after mum very well. He did not like working down the mine, but it was a job, so he took it. I once went for a tour down the mine as part of looking for a job when I left school. I did not like it one bit – underground digging for coal on your knees was not my idea of a job. One benefit from my dad working down the pit, we were given a ton of coal whenever we needed it. My brother and I didn't like the days when the coal arrived as we had to wheelbarrow it from the bottom of the drive up to the coal house – one ton of coal! It took us ages to fill the coal house. It was also our job to rake out the ashes of the fire each morning, put sticks and paper in, and re-light the fire. It meant getting up early, but you can't beat a real coal fire.

Growing up, you might say I was slightly accident prone. One time I was climbing a tree in the nearby woods, when I fell and landed in a big privet bush, three bits of privet got embedded in my leg which meant yet another trip to the hospital to have it all removed. Then there was the time when cycling to school I collided with a car. That resulted in my bike finishing up underneath the vehicle.

Thankfully, although a little battered and bruised, I didn't!

One of my earliest memories of an accident was when I was around two years old, I was being bounced and jiggled on my mother's knee. However, I got a little over excited and jumped off her knee landing head-first on the cast iron surround in front of the fire. My newly formed milk teeth took the brunt of the blow as they were pushed into my gums, some teeth were broken, others were deformed. This greatly affected my speech as from such a young age it was proving difficult for me to form words and sounds, this gave me a massive inferiority complex. I went to school as normal, but had very little confidence when speaking in front of others and as a result, I had to go for elocution lessons until I was 12 to learn how to speak again. My poor teeth were so badly disfigured that by the time I was 17 I'd had them all taken out and false teeth put in. Even now, many years later, I still struggle pronouncing certain words. People who know me well are often surprised that I became a church minister, seeing as it's a calling that involves a lot of public speaking.

Although my parents didn't have much money they looked

after my brother and I very well. Holidays were spent at Bridlington on the East Coast and Matlock Bath in Derbyshire. My Uncle John and Auntie Betty would come too.

Uncle John, Pete, Dave and Dad

While I don't remember my grandparents on my dad's side, I remember well my granddad and grandma on my mother's side. My grandma was a lovely lady, but whether she knew God in a personal way, I know not. My grandma died when I was 13 years old and as a result, my parents made the decision to go and live with granddad. This was not good news for me because he and I did not get on at all. He was not a nice man even though he went to church. Every day he would have a go at me, swear and try to hit me. I remember questioning God about this, as I was often in tears as abuse and anger were thrown at me. I would delay coming home from school if I knew neither of my parents were at home. My life was becoming worse with each day. This went on for a few years. When he died, although it will sound harsh, I have to admit that I was glad.

Grandma Hunt, Pete and Dave

The schools I attended were Barnsley Road Infant School, John Street Junior School and Wombwell High School. I can't remember an awful lot about going to school, but I can remember having fights there and once being pushed through a window. My head was so badly cut that I had to go to hospital. Then another occasion when some of us were messing around in the gym, the teacher gave the entire class the slipper, which with only shorts on, hurt quite a lot. My form teacher had a thick cane and if you messed around or came late to a lesson, he would ask you to bend over, he had an X that marked the spot where we had to bend to, and he would hit you with his cane. On a particularly bad week I was caned seven times!

I enjoyed sports, and always looked forward to games at school. Somehow I managed to get into the school's football team as their goalkeeper. I remember going to a place called 'Jump' to play a game and we lost 4-0. It appeared that I was to blame for all the goals.

My parents attended the Zion Wesleyan Reform Church in the town of Wombwell. My dad served as the youth pastor for some of the time we were at Zion. At this point neither he or my mom had made a pubic declaration of their faith in Jesus, however they would still look after the teenagers and served the Church. It wasn't until years later that they would fully understand and commit their lives to Jesus. You see, the teachings the Zion Wesleyan Reform Church was more based on morals, and how to be a good person. There was very little preaching on the Gospel message, the good news of how God sent Jesus his son to die for us and to bring us into relationship with God. My brother and I were well looked after and even though punishment for wrong-doing was often hard to take, it did not in any way detract from being brought up in a happy home.

Life was good growing up in Wombwell, in those days you could play in the street without fear of being run over. There weren't many cars passing by, during this time they were still a novelty; few people could afford one. Behind our house was a vacant piece of land that had been made into a football pitch. It wasn't a big plot but we could reach it through our back garden. Me and Pete played for many long hours there, often with two friends, Victor and Richard who were our neighbours. There were no goal posts, we would just put our coats down and played. One day Victor, Richard, my brother and I got into a fight with some other local lads. During the fight a lad called David Beaumont threw half a house brick at me and my head was cut badly. I still bear the scar today. We had a Staffordshire dog called Lassie and Victor had a dog called Prince – the brother of our dog. Most Saturdays we would go to the woods with the two dogs and have some fun. Nearby was a canal where we would often swim and mess around. Often the dogs would join us in the water.

There was one day which I have never forgotten, a day that shook my fun carefree days of growing up. A day which from my early years I recognised the power of God's hand on my life. It was when I was about twelve years old, my friend called Leslie came to our house and called for us to see if we wanted to go to the canal. He'd made a home-made boat out of empty barrels and he wanted my brother and I to sail in it with him. We weren't able to go, because my parents had already made plans for us: So just Leslie and Victor went. Later that day we learned that Leslie had gone onto his homemade boat, but it had sunk and Leslie – a non-swimmer, had drowned. I was deeply affected as we were good mates. At his farewell service, I did nothing but cry. But it taught me a great lesson (one I'll reveal later) I still remember his funeral so well, as the previous Sunday all of us lads were together in church. That previous week the preacher had made an appeal for people to respond if they wanted to accept Jesus into their hearts, to become Christians. All the lads except Leslie had made a commitment to be followers of Jesus. He said that he might make that decision next Sunday. Next Sunday never arrived for Leslie. God had kept me from drowning that day for a reason.

That Sunday before Leslie died, was when my life changed forever.   My parents were introduced to three 'evangelists' who were travelling the country holding gospel meetings. My parents had heard great reports about them and so invited them to our church. They preached in a way that the church and my parents had never heard before. They explained how to become a Christian – a true follower of Jesus. They spoke about making a public commitment to serve God, an invitation that I and other members of the church accepted. Their visit brought about great controversy and trouble, because the people in charge of the church at that time did not seem to have much of a concept of God even though they sat on the Church Board. But people heard the good news about Jesus Christ and many made decisions to become Christians. My parents were among those who did that. These evangelists, Gerald Bean, Vic Ramsey and Neville West were God sent people. They also held children's missions in the churches they visited. One such mission for one whole week took place at my church, and I remember well attending those kid's meetings. It was the first time I heard why Jesus had died on a cross; first time I knew that God wanted to live in my life and help me; first time I heard that in order to get into heaven you had to be 'saved'. It was a revelation. It was as if the lights in my heart had just come on. So, when that appeal was given for anyone who wanted to be a Christian to leave their seat and come to the front of the church, I was straight out of my chair and walking to the front. At that time, I was a very quiet, reserved boy because my speech was greatly affected. So, to get me to leave my seat and walk to the front was amazing. As a result of the visit from these three evangelists, my parents, along with my Uncle John and Aunty Betty plus another two relatives – Raymond and Joan Hall all became Christians. Raymond and Joan owned a fruit shop on the High Street in Wombwell. After their encounter that week, from those three evangelists, they felt the call of God on their lives, and later sold up and Raymond went on to become the Pastor of the York Assemblies of God.

My parent's meeting with the three evangelists changed their lives; they found God in a big way. Becoming a Christian changed our home, although life at home was already good, it got even better. That Sunday, right there and then, I told God I was sorry for my sins and I gave my life to God. This was the best decision I had ever made in my entire life.

CHAPTER 2

MY CALLING

After a while my parents were asked to leave the Wesleyan Reform Church because of the conflict of them being there and their desire to do church differently, and so we all started to attend Lundhill Wesleyan Church. The church was at the end of a row of very old houses and surrounded by fields. We were very committed to church and would go three times each Sunday. In those days we had no car, so we would walk. We would leave home around 9:30am, walk for 45 minutes to get to the morning service, then walk back home for lunch. At 2pm we would make the journey again to be present at Sunday school, walk back home and then leave again at 5:30pm in time for the evening service. I can say that I didn't enjoy this as I found church to be boring.

I would sit on the back row along with my brother and mess around, although I had asked God into my life when I was 12, I didn't grow in God at all. The reason being that everyone who came to Lundhill was new in their faith too, so we hadn't had a lot of teaching to help us mature. But my brother and I dare not ask if we could miss Sundays; we were made to go.

Lundhill Wesleyan Reform Church

What made it palatable was the fact that we had a few girls

in the church of our age and they would be messing around during church every Sunday too. I remember how we'd be passing notes to each other and doing other stupid things while the preacher was trying to preach. Sometimes he would stop his talking and tell us to pay attention. My mother, father and Uncle John took up leadership at Lundhill and tried to change things in the church but it was no easy task. Some of the people that came to church, did not want change. My parents had heard of the Assemblies of God and there were a few churches that they knew off in different towns, not too far away. So sometimes we invited guest speakers mainly from Assemblies of God churches to come. I can still remember some of the preachers who visited: Eric Dando, Bob Stephenson, John Philips, David Phillips and John Shelbourne who became my parents' friends.

One night where my life and our church changed forever was when John Philips came and spoke about the Holy Spirit, and taught us about 'speaking in tongues'. All this was new and very interesting to listen to. I had never heard or experienced the presence of the Holy Spirit and was in no way prepared on the power it would have on my life and on my church. I remember John Philips calling a 'waiting meeting' when anyone who wanted to come were welcomed, we would 'wait' for the Holy Spirit to come. The place was full, it was packed, and there was an atmosphere of curiosity as never before had we heard such teaching. In my mind I can still visualise that night. John Philips laid hands on everyone to be filled with the Holy Spirit. That night some amazing things happened, most of the congregation were filled with the Holy Spirit and began to speak in tongues. The church pianist, a young woman called Dorothy, felt the Holy Spirit fall on her and she got onto the piano and her playing was so different, it sounded so good. She hadn't been the best pianist before the Holy Spirit fell, but suddenly she was.

Lundhill was never the same church again. This new experience had brought a new freedom from the religion and routine we had been used to. Church was totally different, there was life there. That evening changed me and my friends, no more were we messing around on the back row. God was in the house, and the church began to grow. However not everyone was pleased with this change and after the leaders of the Wesleyan Reform Union heard about what had happened, and because of the change to our fundamental beliefs, we were asked to leave the Wesleyan Movement as they did not want our church to be affiliated with them. So as a result, Lundhill became an independent church and no longer part of the Wesleyan Reform Movement.

Family gathering at Lundhill Wesleyan Reform Church. (Top right) Dave in his dad's arms with Pete in front.

That night had a profound impact on me, and from reflecting it made me realise that it was from that evening, after I had an encounter with the Holy Spirit, that I began to take my faith more seriously. I began to grow and mature in my faith. One area where I particularly spent a lot of time praying into was what did God want me to do with my life? I had no idea what I wanted to do after leaving school; I had left with no qualifications. I needed direction, I trusted that God would guide me, but at this stage had not really felt God's calling, so threw myself into a variety of professions to see what I could possibly do. There was a man in the church who was self - employed as a builder; he asked if I would like to work with him. He was building a brand-new bungalow. So, for two weeks I carried bricks in a hod up and down stairs. I left as the work was too heavy for me. An offer then came from a printing company in Wombwell to do an apprenticeship in book binding: The firm was Taylor's Printers. I spent six years there doing my apprenticeship, and it also proved to be a place to try and be a real follower of Jesus.

I found it tough going however as in the office I was based was 6 guys and 24 women. I remember my very first day at work, I asked permission to go to the toilet; to get there you had to walk through the print shop where about another 50-people worked. As I was going through the room I noticed that suddenly all the machines were switched off and someone shouted, "There he is, he goes to church, he says he is a Christian." I could have died. Why I got that reaction I don't know, but I went bright red with embarrassment and walked faster to the toilet. Who had told them I know not, but working in the office upstairs was a man called John Shelbourne, a missionary who had to flee for his life whilst working in the Congo. Maybe he had told them. During my 6 years there I was surprised that quite a few people came to talk with me about God and my beliefs.

I enjoyed my time being a bookbinder, although maybe it had something to do with working with so many females! My work was varied, some days I would be setting up on numbering and folding machines, on other days I'd be drilling holes in paper or binding books from scratch. One of the jobs I delighted in doing was to restore the Bible belonging to John Shelbourne. During the Congo uprising, John and his wife, Muriel had to flee for their lives leaving everything behind, including John's Bible. Weeks later a parcel arrived at their house, and inside was his Bible. It was battered, torn and the covers missing. I had the pleasure in taking the Bible to work and could restore it fully. After being at Taylors Printers for six years, my desires began to change, I can't explain fully why but I began to feel unfulfilled at the printers, I felt that God was stirring my heart to do something. I felt the call of God into the ministry. What really helped me understand this was that when I was 17 years of age my father and my Uncle John, who had become joint leaders of the church, now asked me if I would take over the Sunday school. I was over the moon with excitement, but at the same time, scared to death. People had often said I was gifted in working with children so this was the encouragement I needed to see if what they said was true. I accepted. It was from this opportunity to run the Sunday school programme that my first steps in God's plan began.

From that moment, I started I felt that the favour and blessing of God on my ministry. The church was off the beaten track, even more so when the row of old houses came down, but we soon began to grow; not only with the number of kids who had started to come, but with lots of young people and adults who wanted to be part of the team. Sunday school was going very well, so much so, that we decided to run an 'over 10's' event every Monday evening. We decided that it would help us grow more if we went and transported these over 10's to church. Some of the lads had second hand cars and we all offered to help. At one point, we had ten cars going around our town gathering up these youngsters. We even held a competition to see who could get the most children in their car. My brother came out top after squeezing eight kids into his mini! No health and safety experts around then!

It became so popular that the church leadership took a massive decision – to purchase a 53-seater coach. My oh my! The coach became the talk of the town; we were in all the papers, we even got an article in the national newspaper, the Daily Mirror, this was unheard off, to ferry kids to church! Soon every week in our over 10's meetings we were seeing more than 100 youngsters gather together, and God was working in their lives.

During this time, I met John Price who is now the senior pastor at an Assemblies of God church in the Black Country. Occasionally he would come with his band, Lifeline, sometimes for our Pea and Pie Supper events for the over 10's. The band was very good and the band members really related to the kids. Their music was upbeat and the kids loved them.

For some of us we not only had the real excitement of seeing this coach go around our town, but driving the bus ourselves. That was something special; in those days, you did not need a PSV licence as it was classed as a 53-seater car. When it was my turn to drive the coach or to be the conductor, I would come home from work, grab the sandwiches my mother had made, go and pick up the coach and spend the next hour driving around the town picking up the youngsters. Then I'd take the meeting or speak, then drive the kids home again. Such great days! Some of the leaders who were part of the team would always come back to our house. Our house was always full of young people on any night of the week; they would just turn up, unannounced. We had no TV in the house so conversation would be enjoyed by all and most of the time it would be my mum answering the questions these young people wanted answers for. If there were any romances in the air, my mom would always have something to say about who was going out with who and why, very much like a mother hen, protecting and looking after those young people. It was like this most evenings; and it was really good, all of us became great friends. I loved those days! There are many who are still going to church; some serving God, but all of them would want to thank my mom for her input into their lives.

Later, mom and dad loved going to the Assemblies of God conventions and the annual convention was the highlight of their year.

My father and Uncle John took a great risk in encouraging me to lead the kids' work at Lundhill Church but they must have seen something in me to do that. That's one reason why I think mentoring is so very important. To see potential, to see the call of God on someone's life is amazing, and on a one-to-one basis is even better. Although I was feeling God's blessing in the work I was doing with the children, feeling the call of God in my life, was not enough. I remember being taught the biblical way of knowing that it was God calling me. I was in my own church one Sunday, when a member of the congregation came to talk with me and said: "What you are feeling about going into the Ministry, is a God thing, this is the right step for you, follow your heart." I was truly amazed as this person had no idea what I was thinking. I went home very excited. Having told my parents about what this person had said, they responded: "Ask God for more confirmation." They began to explain to me the three-cord principal found in the Bible. (Ecclesiastes ch. 4 v 9-12.) To break a piece of cotton is easy, ask to break two pieces of cotton, much harder, but add another and it's now very hard to break.

You may hear a 'word' from someone. They may have prophesied over you and said things that sounded good. But it's important NOT to just take on board what you have heard and act accordingly, but to ask God for confirmation. I remember going out the following Sunday to another church to speak, and during the meeting there was a message in tongues and the interpretation that followed was almost word for word what had been said to me the previous Sunday. I asked them if they knew the person who had prophesied at my own church, but they did not. So now I had two confirmations. I asked God for another one, knowing that it would be a God thing as a three -fold cord is not easily broken, there is strength now. The third confirmation came two weeks later, when talking to a man who attended my church said: "What you would like to do, do it, because God is in this next step that you are thinking of taking."

CHAPTER 3

VENTRILOQUISM

God had clearly spoken to me through a variety of people, I now knew that serving in children's ministry was what my calling was. I started to experiment with ways to help me put the message of the Gospel over to boys and girls, I decided to try and learn to be a ventriloquist. I put an advert in the local newspaper asking if anyone had a ventriloquist doll that I could use in Sunday school work. The very next day I received a call from a lady who had one in her loft. I went to see her and she gave me the doll for free. For the next three months I sat in front of a mirror learning how to throw my voice. It was hard, very hard and at times I had difficulties with some of my words. When talking normally it was difficult because of how bad my speech was; to throw your voice without moving your mouth was even harder, but I did it. One day I took my doll 'Freddy', to the Sunday school in my own church to give it a go. We had quite some banter between us with Freddy misbehaving especially when he spotted a pretty girl in the congregation. He'd be winking, swiveling his head and generally not paying attention. The people seemed to love it! After a while I bought a much better doll. This one had many more movements – ears, eyes, mouth but its best feature was that it could squirt water from its eyes. So, at the end of my talks I would make the doll cry. Those tears could reach people sitting ten feet away!

Dave and Freddy

After only a few weeks of using the doll at Lundhill, I went away on a Beach Mission to Bridlington for a couple of weeks. I went under the leadership of the 'By All Means' Gospel Trust. In charge was a man called Francis Lammy, who had been doing children's work for a very long time. He also had a ventriloquist doll called Tommy, and he was very good at it, so I watched and learned from the master.

Going on Beach Missions were really something special. Morning and afternoon, we would go on the beach and do 'Sunshine Corner'. We would have around 100 kids come and join us. I used to go every year and spend two weeks of my holidays doing Beach Missions. I went to places such as Chapel St. Leonards, Anderby Creek, Bridlington and Skegness. This was a great training ground for me. Soon my confidence started to increase and slowly I became aware of the anointing of the Holy Spirit that was upon me. This was amazing as I was someone with a massive inferiority complex. I did not think much about myself, my speech problem added to that, so I was always nervous. When in company I was extremely shy. I hated debates, always feeling that everyone was much better than me. In my circle of friends I was not as bad, but meeting others, especially pastors, I was at a loss of what to do or say.

My reputation began to grow and soon I was away most Sundays doing what was called Sunday School Anniversary Specials. Here a big stage would be built inside a church and children would sit and take part in the service: sing a solo, recite a poem, act out a drama and so on. On such occasions the church would always be packed out. These churches were all Wesleyan Reform Churches, which, like my parents' old church, were not used to someone bringing the gospel to them. But we said what we knew to be right. My photo was soon appearing in all the local papers, and then I started to get invites from Assemblies of God Churches. (famous at last!)

I kept a book of where I went and my very first AoG church was Wath-upon-Dearne Church in South Yorkshire, followed by Rossington Church.

The biggest crowd that I ever did my ventriloquist act in front of was the crowning of the Sunday school queen. At this event, which took place every year, there were over

2,000 people present. All the churches in Wombwell would parade around the town and then meet up in a local park to see the crowning of the Sunday school queen.

Freddy aka Dave does some open air preaching

Each church would enter a float on a big lorry for the occasion. We decided to do up our 53-seater coach and stick a giant lollipop on the front. We chose a lollipop because at the end of the kids' meetings we would give everyone a lollipop as they left. The local press got hold of this, so whenever anyone saw this giant lollipop they would know which church we were from.

I remember walking around town on that special day with the streets full of people. My Uncle John decided that as we walked around the town, we would sing songs. Wow! This was not the done thing, but the reaction of the people as we passed them by confirmed without a doubt that we certainly cheered people up.

Procession through the streets of Wombwell

My days in Wombwell were great. I loved speaking to boys and girls about Jesus. D.L. Moody a very famous preacher said this: "If I could re-live my life, I would devote my entire ministry to reaching children with the Good News about Jesus"

I have had the privilege of doing that all through my life, I strongly believe that boys and girls are the church of today. We need to do all that we can to reach children and help them become great followers of Jesus. We worry about what a child will become tomorrow, yet forget that they are someone today.

So at the age of 24 I very strongly felt the call of God to go into the ministry. Even though our church was not part of Assemblies of God, we would go to many of their conventions and events, and that's where I heard about the Assemblies of God Bible College. It was in Surrey, near Croydon and called Kenley Bible College. I filled in an application form and sent if off, thinking that this was my next step. I now felt that God had called me to kids ministry, and so, I felt that I needed qualifications. I was delighted to hear that I had been accepted.

CHAPTER 4

OFF TO BIBLE COLLEGE

I remember leaving home with very mixed feelings. Home was good, I got on well with my parents and brother, I had loads of friends, and church was great too, it was a very active church, but the call of God was so heavy I decided to go. I left my job as a bookbinder and was ready for this next season of my life.

The year was 1969 and I was so excited about going to Bible College, but also very apprehensive. I did not know anyone there and I was no academic. My speech, although a bit better, was on my mind. I still felt that everyone was better than me. My inferiority complex was still a great concern, but the call of God on my life was so strong, I knew it was the right place and the right time to go.

My good friend, Phil Shepherd was going for his first day at a college in Oxford, so I decided to drop him off there first. Unfortunately, we got lost, resulting in me being late and last to arrive at Bible College. Being late did not help me at all, I was shaking inside, scared to death. There were about 40 students, the majority of them male with only a few women.

I was shown to my room which I was to share with a guy called Roger Blackmore. Roger and I became big friends and although he now lives in Long Island, U.S.A. where he is a Senior Pastor, we catch up sometimes on Facebook. He was great to share a room with, he had to stick his feet on the outside of the bed as it was too small, but the 'smell' . . . we won't go there! We had loads of laughs and lots of fun. Roger is a great guy and a man of God.

Me with other students at Kenley Bible College

I remember my room well; it was above the garage and was a very cold room. I had to pile on the blankets to keep warm. College food was okay but supper time most nights would usually be mince. To this day, I can't stand the stuff. The prefect that was over the dorm which Roger and I were in, was a guy called Keith Tipple who as I remember was a very good footballer. Near the Bible College was a place where we could play football, so we often went there to let off steam. We had some laughs during my time there. I made friends with Chris Spicer, Allan Penduck, Peter Butt, Peter Wager and Ian Jennings. We had such people as Aaron Morgan, Elisha Thomson, John Carter and John Whitfield-Foster as our lecturers. Some Sundays we would go and visit Aaron Morgan's church in East Ham, London.

One weekend four of us, Chris, Allan, Ian and I were very late getting back to the college. We knew we would be in trouble if we got caught. You had to be in at a certain time on Sunday evenings. On arriving back at the college, we got a ladder from the garage and put it up to a window that we'd left open. Slowly we made our way up the ladder – only to find the principal of the Bible College, John Carter waiting for us! That wasn't the first time we'd been in trouble, nor was it the last.

It wasn't the place to have fun in, and most of the students would obey the rules, but those mentioned above and myself did our best to enjoy ourselves too. I remember playing cowboys and Indians in the lounge, riding on the seats that had castors on the feet, and Chris Spicer almost running over Elisha Thompson as he was passing through the lounge. Next door to Roger and I in this accommodation block was a young man called Fred, and it was his practice every night to pray aloud before he went to sleep. I remember one night Roger and I decided that the next time he started to pray we would throw objects over the partition onto his bed. Eventually we heard Fred say: "And Lord please bless those who are throwing things at me as I pray."

Although the course was very academic for me, it was great being at the Bible College; we had some great fun as well, learning about Old Testament History, Hermeneutics and Homiletics, Acts of the Apostles. St. John's Gospel and so on. Each week we would have a time of private study where we had to prepare a mini sermon to preach to the students. This was called 'on the block' and the Principal would sit in and listen, then invite you back to his office to tell you how you had done and how best to improve.

Dave (top row centre) and fellow students at Kenley Bible College

Once a year all the students would go to the Assemblies of God Conference, where we were asked to be 'stewards' for the week. We all loved it. In those days, if you were recognized as being at the Bible College; people thought you were important, so much so that we were asked to take

a late night informal meeting that was open to everyone. Every night, there would be around 2,000 people there. I was asked if I would use my ventriloquist doll during the meeting. I did and it seemed to go down well. With my doll, I remember singing a duet with a man called Ernie Crew who was then part of the Executive Council of Assemblies of God, he was a Godly man, but full of fun too. As soon as the 'doll' asked if he would sing with him, there were cheers all-round the room. Sat right in front of me was Pastor Clifford Rees and his wife Mary. I didn't notice at the time that this lady was wearing a suede coat and hat. When I made the doll 'cry', it went all over her. No doubt both hat and coat were ruined. Most people thought it was very funny but whenever I saw the lady afterwards, she would remind me of what I had done, not a happy lady at the time!

Unfortunately, after six months of being in Bible college I began to feel that the course was too academic for me, I had gone there to train to be a better children's speaker and leader however the course content was not specifically on working and ministering to children so I decided to leave Kenley.

CHAPTER 5

WHAT TO DO NEXT?

It was just before the summer holidays, and I was invited to a children's camp in Derbyshire called Bonsall Camp. I was there for six weeks, and found myself helping to run the meetings, organise sports, and other things such as serving meals. It was great.

Ray Belfield and Bob Stevenson were in charge. Both were pastors and so couldn't be at camp all the time. That's where Peter Cunningham came on the scene. He became the leader of the camp and was such a great encourager to me, we got on very well. Peter had such dry humour and his organisation skills were second to none. Together we would run camp, I would be in-charge of the kid's programme and activities whilst Peter oversaw the day to day running like the meals and accommodation.

Bonsall Camp was where I learned so much on how to do kid's ministry better, it was a great training place. But it certainly wasn't the Ritz, in fact it was very primitive. For example, everyone was given a bowl which they would take to the kitchen each morning to fill with cold water from an outside tap, then go back to their tents to wash. When the rain came, many of the tents and chalets would leak. The toilets were situated at the top of a sloping field in a corner, it was a chemical toilet and every night we had to dig a big hole and empty the toilet. Years later a proper toilet was built, with a small room between the gents and ladies, it could sleep two people, it became the place where Pete and I slept. This was a bit of a problem as when anyone went to the toilet in the middle of the night, we'd be woken up by the flush.

The accommodation was not good, very basic in fact. On a few occasions, I had to persuade the kids to get off the coach they had arrived in. They'd take one look at the camp site and wanted to turn around and go back home!

But they stayed and usually came back the following year. It wasn't much to write home about, but it was a place where the blessing and favour of Almighty God was. Only heaven knows how many boys and girls became Christians at this summer camp.

Hundreds of children would come every year, and despite it not being 5 stars (probably not even one star!) the same churches and leaders would come and bring their kids every year.

Dave at Bonsall camp with Chris Spicer

There were many highlights of Bonsall Camp; it was such a great place to spend one's summer. One of the highlights was playing British Bulldog on the sloping field; another was having water fights every Friday. Kids brought their giant water guns along, or they would raid the kitchen for its saucepans. We'd spend hours before the fight making balloon bombs; it was a time when everybody would get soaked. Peter Cunningham would sit on a chair and watch from a distance, but still someone would manage to soak him too!

Bonsall Camp was a fun place to be, even though one morning we were awoken by the sound of a fierce wind. We only realised how bad it had been when we saw it had lifted the roof off our big marquee. Hours later we found it in a field and fortunately managed to sew it back on.

We saw hundreds of boys and girls at camp make the decision to become Christians. A few years ago, I was at the General Conference and, after the Ordination of Ministers' Service, three of the newly ordained Ministers told me they had become Christians at Bonsall Camp.

We had people such as Albert and Peggy Garner with their three kids – Sue, Caz and Paul who would come most years to take a week of meetings, they were a great family, and we always looked forward to their week. Chris Spicer, who was in Bible college with me was a great story teller as he would draw pictures as he was telling his stories. Steve Speight was another guy that came to help us. He is now the Senior Minister at the Assemblies of God Church in Lichfield. We got on very well and shared many camps together.

Another of the highlights was the Wednesday trip. Ray Belfield would come and take charge of these trips. We would normally go to the caves in Castleton. We would always ask for the same guide to take us through the caves, and he'd always get us to sing 'He made the stars to shine, he made the rolling seas, he made the mountains high and he made me.' The voices would echo around the caves for all to hear.

The meetings at camp were always very good; we didn't have problems with the kids who came – not until a young guy called Daniel arrived. I'd had to collect him and some other kids from London in the minibus, and I sensed he wasn't interested in coming to camp. When we made our first stop at a service station, he asked to go to the toilet, on his return, everything seemed normal, but when we were ready to leave, we found that two of the tyres had been let down. We had a good idea who had done it. That first night Peter Cunningham and I were woken by screams and shouts. Someone had cut the guide ropes of the tents and created havoc. It turned out to have been Daniel.

Daniel (right) and other children at Bonsall Camp

He was a very difficult young lad, but we prayed that God would get hold of him and change his life around. His attitude was really bad but on the Thursday night of that week Daniel seemed to be listening to what was being said, and when asked if anyone would like to be a follower of Jesus, Daniel responded and became a Christian and on the Friday we prayed that God the Holy Spirit would come upon him. Now Daniel is serving God at Peter Cunningham's church in Southport and helps run Bonsall Camp today.

Bonsall Camp was the place I first met Paul Weaver and Warwick Shenton, both these young men of God were not known so much in Assemblies of God as they are now, but here they were on camp bringing the kids from their church. (It seems that this is happening less these days, it would be great if more and more churches gave their young people the opportunity to nationally meet with other Christian young people and children).

I was awoken at 6am on the Sunday morning after Paul Weaver had arrived with their kids. The noise was coming from the football field just a few feet where Peter and I slept. On opening my door, I saw Paul Weaver and the kids playing football. But this was Sunday! God's day, a day of rest, it was the Sabbath. We did not play ball games on a Sunday. But we did after Paul's visit! I will never forget Bonsall Camp, a great training place for me, encouraged by Peter Cunningham I began to embark on a great journey.

CHAPTER 6

ON THE MOVE TO NEW PLACES

My next season in life was about to begin. After spending six weeks on camp I found myself travelling up to Scunthorpe after being invited by Paul Weaver to conduct a week's event for children at his church. This was to be the start of four years travelling around the UK holding kids' events for a week at a time at various churches. During my time in Scunthorpe, Paul got me to go on the radio – I was nervous, so I took 'Freddy' along and between us we got through the radio interview!

Those four years were so special; God seemed to be anointing my ministry as invitation after invitation came my way. I remember going to such places as Sunderland, Newcastle, Wigston, Dartford, Bristol, Dalton, Dudley, Canterbury, Malvern, Rotherham, Worcester, Stoke on Trent, Whitehaven, Walthamstow, Gateshead, Ripon, Bawtry, Blackburn, Maltby, South Normanton,

Rossington, Bentley, Moston, New Moston, Royston, Hartlepool, Seaham, Havercroft, Lincoln, Horden, Croyden, Camden Town, Brownhills, Hounslow, Swallownest, Peckham, Bell Green, Kersley, Crayford, Wath, Maidstone, Denton, Purley, Alfreton, Newport, Wigan, Newtown, Kirkby, Prestatyn, Wirksworth, Newstead, Exeter, Chesterfield, Mansfield, Woodhouse, to name but a few.

Prestatyn was the place when I realised that I needed to keep humble as I travelled the UK, because on the second night of our kids' event as Warwick and I drove into the church parking area, it was full of kids, loads of them, they were shouting my name as if I were famous.

That night in Warwick's home I remember as if it were yesterday, kneeling down and asking God to help me always to be humble and to give God thanks at all times. We may be gifted in many areas, but if we go in our strength, we will fail. What we all need in ministry is to know the Anointing of the Holy Spirit upon us, without that, not much will happen, it would be mere words and a lot of fun, but with the Anointing, you will see life changing moments.

One of the other places that I remember so well, was South Normanton, a good church and again I was asked to go into the local schools to take part in their assemblies. I was also asked to speak at the senior school and I invited them to come to the youth meeting at the church on the Friday.

We counted 80 people that turned up that night to join the young people that were already part of the youth. I was asked to speak and I remember three young people coming to the front to become Christians, and as far as I know they are still following Jesus and going on with God today.

In Sunderland we held our kids' event for a week. At that time Sunderland was one of the most high ranking churches in AoG. We had been offered their minor hall, which was quite a big space, but it was soon full, so permission was asked to use the main church hall. I remember we had to move anything that could be spoiled, stolen or made a mess of before we could use the church, but we filled the church. To speak at such churches as Sunderland was indeed a great honour. Wherever I went, we would always pack the church out; we would always see kids giving their lives to God. That was always the highlight of the week.

Every year I was invited to Moston and New Moston in Manchester. The 'Mother' Church and their 'Sister' Church. The Senior Minister was Paul Newberry, a great man of God. I always looked forward to these two weeks. I stayed in Paul and Pat's home with their three girls. He was such a Godly man, full of fun too and a great encouragement to me. To have me every year in his church was amazing. Each night we ran the kids' meeting, we would go around the streets with a giant tug of war rope, and kids would see us coming, get hold of the rope, and we took them to the church. You would not be able to do that today. Paul had been an Associate Minister under Pastor Fred Weaver in Birmingham and before I too went to Birmingham, Paul wrote a letter to me and gave me great advice about my role in Birmingham. Sadly, Paul is not with us today, as he died quite young, yet another 'Why' came from my heart, why God, why?

Another church where I used to go quite often was Dartford; the man of God in those days was Veyne Austin.

They too would bring their kids to Bonsall Camp. Today he has a great family working for God in different places, some abroad. I fondly remember these men.

Inspiring kids even in my senior years

After four years on the road travelling around the UK, my diary wasn't as full as it used to be and I remember very clearly driving back home one Sunday evening. Travelling up the M1 my car suddenly broke down, the 'big ends' had blown. When I finally got home hours later I was somewhat deflated, depressed and wondering where God was in all this. For four years, life was really good, I had met many people and made many friends. I saw hundreds of kids make decisions to become Christians. I had been in many schools talking about Jesus. The anointing of the Holy Spirit was upon me, my ministry was on a high, but was it to all end abruptly and go pear shaped?

CHAPTER 7

DIFFICULT TIMES

I remember questioning God. Was His calling just for a season, and was this the end? My brother Peter said that I ought to look for a job, so I started to work for Betterware, the job was to go from house to house trying to sell things like brushes, car wash stuff, ironing board covers etc. My first day was a disaster. It was November, snow was on the ground, it was very cold, and for eight hours I went from house to house without selling a single thing. So, I went back the next day and quit.

My family were not impressed with my actions at all, right then I was at my lowest point in my life, I remember my brother Pete having strong words with me. Then about a week later I was in town looking around, when I met my old boss at the printing firm, she informed me that the guy that took my place when I left the company, had himself left two days ago, so I was asked if I wanted my old job back. So, the following week I went back to my job of book binding. But I was still feeling confused, hurt and depressed. I was questioned by those at work who knew me, asking what had gone wrong? They remembered that when I left to go to Bible College four years ago I'd felt it was for life. So, what had gone wrong? I had no explanation.

Even though I had a few invitations to carry out, and I got back into the kids' work at my local church, I was still wondering all the time, where was God? It seemed like I was back to square one. Those times were very difficult for me, I remember on more than one occasion crying, asking the question, 'Why God, why?'

After about a year, a friend of my father, Mr Randerson, died. Mr Randerson had a cobbler's shop nearby, mending shoes. My brother and I decided to buy the shop and turn it into a shoe shop. I would leave my job and run the business of selling shoes. I must admit I was a little lost, was selling shoes what I was going to do for the rest of my life? Did God want me to be a shoe shop owner?

The place was extremely small, not much room to swing a cat. But my Aunty Betty (wife of my Uncle John) came and dressed the window, set out the shoes, and we were open for business. We called it, the not very original 'Dave's'.

We paid £1,500 for the shop, which was quite a bit of money in those days. So, each day I would open up 'Dave's' but business was not brilliant; I had really no idea what I was doing. Reps would come in and try and sell me every shoe that was available. I remember that I would sell more Doc Martin boots than anything. There was a junior school opposite my shop, one day some kids came in, so I brought out Freddy and put a little show on. As a result, my shop was full of kids most nights after that. I have no idea if any went on to become Christian, I can only hope. Having the store packed out with the children gave me confirmation that my calling had not left me, that God still had something for me to do.

After about a year, out of the blue, I received an invitation to go to the West Midlands to a big children's event at Dudley Town Hall. The place was packed with boys and girls and what I did seemed to go down well. The following week I received a letter from a Pastor Fred

Weaver, the Senior Pastor at Calvary Temple Church in Balsall Heath, Birmingham.

In the letter, he said that he thought I had done very well at the kids' event and wondered if I was interested in coming to Birmingham to be their full time youth and children's pastor. I was over the moon, so excited, but at the same time, scared to death. Although I knew Paul Weaver I did not know his father, nor did I know anyone from the church. So, my brother and I sold the shoe shop – for the same amount that we paid for it, £1,500 and I prepared for the next chapter in my life.

CHAPTER 8

BIRMINGHAM HERE I COME!

I arrived one Saturday in Birmingham and was introduced to the couple who were going to look after me – Joe and Gert. They were such good people. Joe was a deacon in the church and 'Aunty' Gert did a lot of work behind the scenes; both are now in heaven. Their daughter, Pauline served as a leader of the church for many years up to recently. She was a devoted faith-filled Christian who worshipped and was thankful to God all the way to her last breath.

Pastor Weaver asked me what I would like the people to call me. I didn't understand the question, so I said: "My name is Dave!" Mr Weaver explained that I ought to be called 'Pastor Lakin'. I did not like that one bit. It seemed so formal and I felt older than my 28 years. I would not have minded 'Pastor Dave', but it wasn't to be. Pastor Lakin it was. Pastor Weaver was a very Godly man, a great teacher of the Bible and the church had grown since he and

Mrs Weaver arrived at Calvary Temple. He was very strict, not always easy to talk to and would expect what he said to be carried out. My very first task was to wallpaper my office which was 'up in the gods' right at the very top of the church. There was nothing there; it was used as a store room. I had never done any wallpapering in my life, and had no idea how to start. So, my very first week was spent wallpapering what was to become my office. I didn't know what was expected of me and Pastor Weaver was so busy I didn't see much of him during my first few weeks.

Those weeks were extremely hard, and became even harder when I found out that they already had a youth leader who had no idea what I had come to do. He thought he was over me and I thought I was the man in charge. The trouble was that although Pastor Weaver had made it clear to me that I was now the youth leader, this man thought differently. After a few eventful months, he left the church with his family. Not a great start to my full-time ministry! It caused a bit of a storm within the youth department and it took a long time before I felt that I was the Youth Pastor.

The church had bought an old cinema in Bromsgrove which was badly in need of renovating. So, for quite a few months, I would travel to Bromsgrove with Pastor Weaver and others to be a labourer. For months, I was kept busy making concrete and wheeling it to where it needed to go. Although very tired I was still expected to attend all the meetings that were happening, and there was more than a few of them!

We had Silver Lining which was a meeting for the elderly on a Tuesday afternoon; prayer meeting in the evening; Wednesday evening there was a children's event;

Thursday night was Bible study; and Friday evening was the youth meeting. Most Saturdays we would take the young people out somewhere, so the only night I was not in church was a Monday.

When I arrived in Birmingham, I noticed a very attractive young lady, who was the leader of a weekly Bible class for young people and who loved God. Her name was Lesley and besides being very attractive, she was also a very gifted young lady. I heard that she had been to the same Bible college as me, Kenley Bible College.

Lesley was very friendly with one of Pastor Weaver's daughters – Joyce, and together they ran their own business – a baby wear shop. Joyce was going out with a guy called Allan Penduck, who was at the Bible College when I was there. We first met when Allan and Joyce Weaver came to Wombwell for the weekend to spend time with me, and they asked if Lesley could come too. Although she had rang my bell, I don't think I rang hers. She did not like my Yorkshire way of doing things, so from the start we just did not get on.

I did some stupid things in my first few months, which

also caused me not to be able to get close to Lesley. One of the things that I messed up big time was to shut down all the Sunday schools that were around the city and transport them all to one church. At that time, each Sunday school was doing well, we had about five branch Sunday schools, reaching around 200 kids each week. I thought it best to bring them all under one roof, but it was a big mistake.

Lesley was not at all happy with that decision, and said it was the wrong move. She was right. And I possibly made the worst decision that I had made in the church whilst a Youth and Children's Pastor.

After a while Lesley began to melt a little, it must have been my charm that did it! So much so that after 10 months we were married. We were both 28 years of age – a great age to get married. Naturally we married at Calvary Temple, it was good to have Pastor Weaver marrying us, and my Uncle John speaking at the wedding.

Once a married man I left Joe and Aunty Gert's home and we set up our own home in King's Heath, Birmingham. We found that we were struggling to pay our way; I was not on a high salary so I decided to ask the leadership if I could go part time and have two jobs. This was agreed and I found work delivering bread and cakes around the city. I had to be there at 6am each morning, sometimes including Saturdays; I would then load my deliveries of bread and cakes, and return back to the bakery for 12 noon. I then went home and had a little lunch as I had to be back in church by 1pm. Leave again at 5pm, but back again for 7pm every night except Monday.

Dave, Lesley, Pastor Fred Weaver and Uncle John

Then tragedy struck. It was June 1975 and I was sitting at home in Birmingham, watching ITV National News. The headline news that evening was about a gas explosion at the Houghton Main Colliery. It said that there were many miners still unaccounted for. I phoned my mum and she said that dad was at the mine, and she had not heard from him but my brother Pete had gone to see what he could find out. The next morning at 2am, my brother phoned to say that dad had been killed in the explosion. He was one of five miners to lose their lives that night.

That question we all ask when things like this happen in our lives is 'why God, why?' I still trust God even though at times I do not understand Him. For four weeks after this event I was very angry at God, my daily devotions were not happening. I still went to church, I even preached but I found it so hard to praise God, I just turned off in regard to God, Church, and Ministry. Here I was serving God, yet God had let this happen I felt.

My favourite verse was and still is Romans ch. 8 v 28. Where God had promised that all things would work together for good – but I could see no 'good' in my dad's death. I was extremely angry, hardly slept and I had a very bad attitude. Every day was a bad day.

My good friend Chris Spicer came to see me at church. I was busy cleaning the Minor Hall. Chris began to talk to me about the Sovereignty of God and it's times like these that one has to trust God. Slowly the anger began to subside, slowly I began to read and pray again, slowly I once again started to love God.

My dad, Irving Lakin

Some good did come out of my dad's death – as I remember being at the Bonsall Camp a few weeks after this tragedy. Each week for three weeks we had children who had come on camp because their mum or dad had died, so I was able to sit down with them and share what was in my heart and help them with their grief.

I mentioned before how Pastor Weaver was a man of discipline and sometimes difficult to work with, but it's what I needed in my life then, and for the ministry in general. He stood no nonsense and if he thought I needed a telling off, I probably did. Sometimes though I was reduced to tears. It was hard at the time to take, but stood me in good stead for the 19 years later in life when I was the Senior Minister.

After being the youth pastor for 12 months I felt tired and jaded, not being as effective as I should have been in my role at church. One day whilst in church I collapsed and was sent home immediately. The leadership then met and decided that I should not go back to the bakery, but whatever I was being paid at the bakery, the church would now pay me. So once again I was the full-time Youth and Children's Pastor.

Then something wonderful happened for Lesley and I, our first son, Simon was born on 4th October 1976. Three years later we were blessed with another son, Daniel who came along on 20th August 1979.

Lesley, Daniel and Simon

CHAPTER 9

HAPPY DAYS

For 16 years I was the youth and children's pastor and we had some really amazing times. Numerically, we were growing, and also we saw lots of the young people growing in God. Having fun was always a priority and our Monday night youth meetings each month would consist of three weeks of us worshipping God, listening to the word of God being preached, and trying to teach the young people how to walk with God each day. Then on the last week of the month we would have a social night. Maybe it would be a games night, a quiz night or we would book a gym and play 5 -a-side football, soft ball or activity games. We would also bring in top youth speakers. People such as John King, Ian Green and Peter Wildrianne would also speak. At one point, we seemed to have the biggest youth group in AoG.

The church bought a 53 seater coach, and on many a

Saturday we would take teenagers to places like Newport, Scunthorpe, Bristol, Yorkshire, and meet up with their young people. The lads would play a football match against the other church, and the girls would play a netball match, then we would all enjoy a buffet together, followed by a youth service. Those were great days. The young people made lots of new friends.

I remember us going to Newport to see my friend Omri Dando, the son of Eric Dando who was very well known in Assemblies of God. In fact, he became part of the Executive Team, and sometimes Chairman at the General Conference. On one of these occasions I was to speak at the end of our day of activity, and to my surprise, Eric Dando came to listen. I was very nervous of preaching in the first place, but seeing Mr Dando made me doubly nervous. I remember how he got a chair and sat directly in front of me on the front row. Afterwards he shook my hands, so I imagine I did okay!

After a few years, we were seeing over 100 young people coming on a Friday night. One of our challenges was to try and get them to also come to church on a Sunday morning.

We wanted the youth department to be a place where anyone could come and feel welcome. We would preach against 'cliques' and tried to make sure that no one felt left out. If someone had a birthday, we encouraged them to invite all the young people to their party. If someone was going somewhere, then they were asked to ring around everybody to see if they wanted to go too. Whenever we went out on a Saturday, we would make sure that everyone was invited.

Music was not such a big deal at that time, all we had on the platform at the church was an organ and a piano. No drums or guitars were allowed; we had no worship singers and 99.9% of the time we would sing hymns but no choruses. Pastor Weaver would often lead the meeting with his accordion.

One important point that I need to make is that Pastor Weaver was very supportive towards what we were trying to do, but at the same time thought that because our numbers were so large, he could see a church within a church. At that time, the youth department were better off financially, while other departments at times were struggling. It seemed that the young people would put their offerings in on a Friday night at the youth meetings rather than in the Sunday morning collection. We had to teach them the principles of tithing.

The youth from those days are still serving God today, most are still in the same church. There are many people who were nine, ten and eleven years old in those days, who today are married, have children, and are still in the house of God serving Jesus in the UK and abroad. Names that spring to mind include Vince and Debbie Ricketts, Bradford and Louison Ricketts, Vernon and Sharon Dore, Pat Lake, Sharon Davis (nee Mullin) and Carmelita to name a few.

Some of the named were also leaders of a program called The Royal Rangers. It was during my time as the Youth and Children's Pastor that we noticed that around the country many churches were getting involved in this uniformed organisation called Royal Rangers. It was very strong in the U.S.A and in other countries such as Australia, so we decided to join. Although in the States it was a 'boys only' ministry, we decided that it would be open for the girls too.

Royal Rangers became an overnight success in our church. We had loads of boys and girls attending each week, and they loved it. We would do a parade where the children would line up in their age groups, each week they would say aloud the Royal Ranger Pledge which is: With God's help I will do my best to serve God, my church, and my fellow man; to live by the Ranger Code; to make the Golden rule my daily rule. Then we would salute the Commanding officer and pray over the lives of all those that came.

We made visits to the local Police Station, also to the Fire Station, sometimes we would go outside to play team games.

Twice a year we would go camping for the weekend which was great fun. I remember our first camping trip, we arrived one Friday evening in our church coach, only to find that it was raining very hard, we left the kids in the bus while most of the leaders went out in the pouring rain to put up all the tents.

We were blessed with many leaders and over the many

years that we did Royal Rangers, it was really something special as we saw lots of boys and girls go on to become leaders in the Rangers themselves. I believe that there will be many children who became a Christian in Royal Rangers and one day we will meet again in Heaven.

Royal Rangers parade with Lukas Dewhurst, Dave and Billy Richards

Another way of reaching young people which I think is so important is by giving them the opportunity to socialise and spend time with each other. So, for many years whilst being a youth pastor I organised camps (retreats) where young people could have fun, create great memories and listen to the word of God. The camps I ran were mainly for groups of young people from churches that I knew very well, in places such as Scunthorpe, Newport, Bristol, and Birmingham. For 12 years I and others organised such camps, and for nine of those years we were at The Gaines Christian Youth Centre in Herefordshire.

The Gaines complex was a great place to go; it had accommodation for around 120 young people. It had an indoor swimming pool, football pitch, horse riding etc. Talking about horse riding, one year I decided that I would go horse riding, Paul Weaver came too. I don't know what happened, maybe a wasp stung my horse making it bolt but suddenly there I was hanging onto the horse for dear life, heading straight for some trees and shrubbery. Then abruptly, the horse just stopped and I went flying over the bushes. I escaped with a dislocated elbow. I've never been back on a horse since. But our nine years there were really good. We seemed to get the same churches and the same young people coming each year.

Then for another three years we went to the Lake District to a camp called Blaithwaite House, which was another great venue for camps. Accommodation wise, it was like the Gaines, having about 120 beds. I remember one year going there with the young people from Calvary Temple and we travelled up on the church's 53¬ seater coach.

So, we had 53 people on board plus their luggage and all the food for the week, as we were self-catering. As we reached the Lake District we began to climb a very steep hill, Lennox, the driver, shouted out to me, "I don't think we will get up this hill." So very quickly, while the coach was still moving, we had to get all the young people off, go to the back of the bus, and push. I am sure that God was with us that day, as the coach could easily gone backwards down the hill and crashed.

Also, that same year we took the coach to a seaside place near to where the camp was. As we drew near we saw lots of cars parking on the sand, so we decided to join them. Unfortunately, the coach was too heavy and it sank into the sand. We had to buy shovels to dig our way out.

For those 12 years, we had as our speakers Warwick Shenton and Paul Weaver. No doubt about it these men of God were anointed to bring the word of the Lord, we saw many become Christians, many were filled with the Holy

Spirit, and the teaching of Paul and Warwick was awesome. We never thought about having different speakers, as their ministry was complementary to each other. Jenn Weaver and Cynthia Shenton would always come to camp too with their husbands.

Even today there are many of those young people still serving God, all because of the teaching and encouragement that those two men brought. Twelve years at youth camp, amazing times.

CHAPTER 10

SMOKING HOT OPPORTUNITIES

Every year we would go to the Assemblies of God Conference, where for one night I would be asked to speak to all the boys and girls who were at the conference with their parents. I always looked forward to this. Colin Benton was the man in charge and one day he asked me if I would like to do this instead of him and organise the whole week. Wow! What an honour and a privilege to be asked. In those days, the Annual General Conference was the place to go, they were held in such places as Bognor Regis, Prestatyn and Minehead. The Conference was attracting over 6,000 attendees. This was the place to be! The General Conference, what a great holiday that was!

Loads of young people would go, and we had some great fun. At times our 'fun' got out of hand, we would stay up very late and often get into mischief. One evening Omri and I decided to go to the boating lake which had an island in the middle. We changed into some old clothes, got into the water and untied every boat. Then we took them over to the island and secured them there. So, when they came back in the morning they would have to walk through the lake to get their boats back!

One time we were messing around in the early hours of the morning and we got caught by the 'Night Patrol'. We were told that we would have to be dealt with by the Executive Council that afternoon. Omri was petrified about the meeting as his dad was on the Executive Council and who also happened to be the Chairman of the Conference that year. His dad's face was a picture when he saw his son. And maybe we'd have been sent home had it not been Eric Dando that met with us. Thankfully, I could carry on doing the kid's activities the following year. Mr Dando had perhaps forgotten what happened at the previous year's conference.

We would get around 200 kids attending each night. I could pick my own team and invite who I wished to speak, but everyone had to pay their own way. Because I strongly believe that boys and girls are the church of today, I felt that not enough was being done to minister to these kids. There was no budget, there was no promoting the kids' meetings, and it seemed to be just a 'babysitting' exercise. No recognition of what was happening each night with the boys and girls, you did what you could, but the kids' activities were very poor.

But one year all that changed, because appointed onto the Executive Council of AoG were Paul Weaver and Warwick Shenton. They asked to speak to me regarding the children that came to the conference with their parents. As a result, there was a massive improvement in what had been happening. For example, the kids' meetings were advertised in the posters and leaflets concerning the conference which were being sent out. My team and I were all paid for; the team were given the tapes of all the speakers that spoke during the week; we could give out good prizes and put big posters all around the venue advertising the kids' meetings. We were also asked to do some craft work and fun activity games in the mornings.

Tony Williams from Coventry Church made some fabulous props, games, and brilliant posters. We became great friends and still are to this day. What Warwick and Paul achieved was unheard of. For the first time, children were put where they ought to be, on a par with adults. We even had the conference chairman coming in on the first night to welcome all the youngsters. Thanks to Paul and Warwick for changing the ways children were thought about and their importance in church today.

On the Sunday afternoon of the conference week, there was an all age Sunday school. On one of these occasions I was asked to speak and decided to tell the story of Elijah on Mount Carmel. I hired a pantomime bull to come down from the back of the room ready to be killed. Inside the bull were Paul Weaver and Allan Penduck. I was Elijah and the prophets of Baal were Bob Stevenson and Paul Finn.

We had rehearsed how we were going to produce fire. Each of the prophets of Baal had a small container of petrol and were asked to sprinkle just a little on the altar that we'd made. Then, when I started to pray, I had a match in one hand and a match box in the other. I was to strike the match and throw it on the altar. We had practiced this back home in Birmingham many times. However, the prophets of Baal got carried away and poured out the entire contents of their containers onto the altar. So much so that when I stuck the match and threw it on the altar, a massive fire ball shot up and almost set fire to the stage's velvet curtains. As people ran to get fire buckets, the kids just howled with laughter, thinking it was all part of the story. I was never asked again to tell that story!

For some reason, I don't have much luck with fire! In fact, I remember the first Cremation service I was involved in. Pastor Weaver was away one time in America. While he was away, someone in the church died. He said that I would have to take the service which was firstly in church, and then everyone was to go to the crematorium for the committal. I had not done one before or been part of this kind of a service. But I had noticed that whenever there was a Thanksgiving Service for someone who had died, the West Indian community would always support it. The church would always be full, and not only in the church but at the graveside or crematorium too. If it was a burial, they would come prepared to sing, and after the committal wanted to fill in the grave themselves.

The Church service went well but arriving at the crematorium, the man came to explain what I had to do. He pointed out three buttons beside the pulpit. One button to play the music, another to draw the curtains and the third to send the coffin down. Although the service in the church went well, I made big mistakes at the crematorium. The first button I pressed sent the coffin down, the second played the music and the third closed the curtains. If people noticed my mistake, they were kind enough not to say anything.

A further example of the unlucky relationship with fire was when we had a baptismal service and before we got into the baptism tank we made sure that we'd switched the heating of the tank off. I forgot to do this one baptismal night after we'd had around 15 people being baptised.

Pastor Weaver said to me on a couple of occasions whilst standing in the tank, "The water is getting very warm." But we just carried on. After the last one had been baptised, we went into Pastor Weaver office to change, it was then that I noticed that he looked like a boiled lobster. Not surprisingly he complained of not feeling well. I quickly fetched Mrs Weaver. The baptistery was of course too hot, so I got into big trouble that night!

Unfortunately, I didn't learn from that mistake, because one Sunday evening at another baptismal event, I again forgot to switch off the heat in the tank, so we baptised people and closed the service. Boards were placed over the baptistry area and we all went home. I was awakened in the middle of the night by the police, saying that they thought the church was on fire, could I come quickly with the keys. When I got inside you could not see anything except smoke. We quickly took off those boards, to find that elements inside the tank had been destroyed. Every baptismal after that Sunday, we had to hire in heaters to heat up the water. It was an expensive mistake to make. I wish that was all the stories I had to tell in terms of setting things on fire, my experiences don't just include church life but at home too. Way back in November 2011 I was cooking myself some tea, I took my chips out of the chip pan and went to settle down to watch the TV. Whilst I was tucking away I heard whizzing and banging sounds. I thought, they are a little late for bonfire night, and carried on eating when I heard a louder bang from the kitchen. I got up to investigate what these sounds were when I saw huge flames coming from the chip pan, I had accidently placed the empty chip pan, full of oil, back onto the hob which I had forgotten to switch off. I instinctively grabbed the handle and ran outside as I opened the patio door the wind blew the oil over my hand and face which resulted in a trip to A&E. To say Lesley was not happy was an understatement as we had just had all our lounge redecorated. In the end, we were out of our house for about 4 months which went over Christmas whilst we had to have our house redecorated and a new kitchen fitted because of all the smoke damage.

Anyway, back to leading the kids' activities at conference was indeed an honour. And it was a pleasure and a delight to have the kids for the whole week. People gave up their holidays to be part of the kids' team. We all wore matching jumpers and some years we would be asked into the main conference hall to sing to everyone. For many, many years we were responsible for all the kids' activities for the whole week.

However, the next invitation that came my way blew me

away. It was from Ian Green, who was the National Youth Alive leader. He was in-charge of nationally bringing young people together by organising a variety of rallies and events. It was an opportunity for young people from all over the country, from a variety of churches to meet up and make connections and friendships with other Christians and give them the bigger picture that there are more like minded followers of Christ in the world other than those in their own churches. In the 1990's when social media was none-existent and communication was not as rapid, this was a crucial way of young people being able to engage and meet with others. Ian Green asked me if I would like to come on the Youth Alive National Team. It had to go to a vote at conference, but I got enough votes to get me onto that prestigious team, I was over the moon as I passionately believed in everything they did for the young people. On the team with Ian were Alan Hewitt, Ken Williamson, Mark Sherratt, Steve Ritchie and Peter Wildrianne. This was the start of really enjoying my time on the council. I was there for 10 years, during that time, Alan Hewitt became the chairman of Youth Alive, he was a Godly man and he would always start our meeting together as a team by giving us a devotion, which often was part of what he had spoken about the previous Sunday at his church. We all sat with eyes wide open, quickly writing down what he had to say, so that we could preach some of it the next Sunday in our local churches!

There were many, many highlights during my 10 years on Youth Alive. We would do two rallies each year, all in the major cities of the UK. We would organise training events; we ran youth camps and 'missions' abroad; two NEC events, all the fund-raising for various projects; having our own National Youth Conference evening events at the General Conferences. Those 10 years were awesome years. London, Manchester, Leeds, Birmingham, Newport, Leicester, Sheffield, Bristol and many other venues holding around 2,000 were booked. Before I came on the Youth Alive Team I was someone that lacked confidence. I had a massive inferiority complex, I thought everyone was better than me. When I met people of importance I would almost 'bow' when I met them, but thankfully being part of this team made me understand that we are all the same, we just have different strengths, different skills and gifting. That's why it's called 'Team' so that together we can make something good happen.

The biggest event that the we put on were the events at the NEC. Peter Wildrianne and I were asked to organise these. Part of my role was to sell and distribute the tickets. I was given a massive layout of all the seats on paper and every day when tickets were asked for I would fill in the blank places. Each day I would dash to my post box when I heard the postman come. It was very exciting filling in all the blank boxes. First time around we filled the main hall at the NEC – it seated 12,000. What a great sight to see 12,000 young people praising God.

All the young people from Calvary Temple were stewards for the day. This first event at the NEC had speaker Reinhard Bonke. People from all different organisations came for the day as we had afternoon and evening meetings. All around the NEC we had many stalls from different ministries, all of them with something to offer young people.

On one evening service there was a lady called Jean Neil who had come in a wheelchair, I remember seeing Reinhard place his hand on this lady's head and while praying suddenly by the power of God, she got up out of her wheelchair and began to walk around the area. What a great miracle 12,000 people had witnessed! They went wild as they saw Jean Neil going home pushing an empty wheelchair. Wow! What a day that was! I will never forget it and neither will those 12,000-young people. We took £20,000 in the two offerings and the Youth Alive Team then decided to give it all away to various ministries within Assemblies of God.

For the second event at the NEC a year later we had invited Arthur Blessed to be our guest speaker for the day. He had become 'famous' for carrying a big wooden cross around the country. But just a few weeks before the event he sent us a message to say that he had left his wife, but was still willing to come and preach. But we cancelled his visit and invited Laurence Singleton from 'Youth With A Mission' to be our speaker. But we were disappointed on two accounts, one because of the change of speaker, and secondly, we only had 10,000 young people booked in.

Mark Sherratt, the Senior Minister at the Milton Keynes Christian Centre was now on the Youth Alive Team and at a Youth Alive rally in Manchester, Mark arranged for me to come on to the stage on a Harley Davidson motor bike, to ride out with my leather jacket and sunglasses on, just to give the notices for the day. The crowd went crazy. (Famous at last!)

Because of being on the National Youth Alive team, I was invited to be part of the organising team for the National Assemblies of God Conference, which meant that I would be in meetings with lots of men that were then part of the Leadership of AoG. Being someone who had very low self-esteem and a massive inferiority complex, to be sat with these men was difficult for me. But the more times we met, the more confident I became in my own gifting and skills and I realised that these men were just like me, we just had different skills. I still don't like being in small groups with other Ministers, there is still a feeling that others are better than me. I would much rather preach in front of 200 people, than to be sat in a small group of Ministers having some debate.

When I became part of the Youth Alive Team, the guys on the team wanted to run a Youth Alive camp, and I was asked by the team to try and organise something. We were offered a school in East Sussex called Great Walstead, a great venue, with large playing fields, outdoor swimming pool, forest and a chapel. There was already a youth camp there which was run by Peter Butt who had been in Bible College with me. He kindly allowed us to have three weeks when the school was on its summer break.

It was agreed that Ken Williamson who was part of the Youth Alive Team, should run and organise the first week and that I should run and organise the last two weeks. We had some great camps whilst at Great Walstead. I imagine some readers may remember the football and cricket games we had, not forgetting the infamous midnight walks.

It was a great opportunity to bring in young men to speak. We had John Partington, John King, Keith Tipple, Ian Green, Simon Jarvis, Alan Hewitt and Roger Blackmore. All of them were gifted in speaking to young people. No doubt there are many today who came to the Youth Alive camps who have great memories of the place. We would have around 600 young people over the three weeks at camp each year, and Heaven will reveal how many lives were changed by the power of God. It's true what is often said about camp: young people gain more from camp weeks than they do in 12 months at their local church. A problem we had at Great Walstead was that before camp started we had to put beds and mattresses into every classroom, and put them back at the end of camp. Two hundred beds and mattresses took us a long time to take out of storage and then put back. One year we needed help so badly that we hired a tractor with a trailer. Richard Blower, from the Bedworth Church, drove the tractor otherwise we would have been there much longer. We couldn't leave the school until it had been inspected by the School Trustees. I remember one year how they would not allow us to go home until around 6pm, they kept on finding fault. One of the main features of the school was their beautiful chapel, so it was a delight to go to the meetings. Sadly, the school decided that we couldn't use their venue anymore, so we gave youth camps a miss the following year.

I can recall some pranks that happened at youth camp. For example, how someone put a banana up the exhaust of

John Partington's car, so when he moved off we got showered in banana. Many of the pranks were down to John Partington. He and John King even dropped a stink bomb during an evening appeal. Angry I went looking for them and found John King hiding in a wardrobe.

Another time, John Partington persuaded all the young people to applaud the minute Alan Hewitt got up to speak. It went on for quite some time and got so bad that I had to call a halt to what was happening. Then there was the time he threw water over everyone half way through his message. And even cut up a baby doll and threw the bits and pieces of the doll into the congregation.

You always had to be on your guard whenever you are with John as he would do and say things that were unexpected. I remember another occasion being sat in a District Minister's meeting with John, the venue was Calvary Temple. Half way through the business side of this John put his hand up to speak to the Chairman. Being given permission, John stood and said: "Mr. Chairman, I am bored, can we do something different?" His request was turned down!

Yes reader, the same John Partington who has for the last 8 years been serving as National Leader of Assemblies of God. There are many more stories like these about Mr Partington. If you need to know more – ask me!

CHAPTER 11

PUTTING ON A BIGGER JACKET

I had spent 16 years as the Youth and Children's Pastor, when Pastor Weaver decided that he would step down as the Senior Minister. During Pastor Weaver's time, many had been converted, baptised in water and baptised in the Holy Spirit, and many are still going on with God today. He was a demanding man to work with at times. I remember on more than one occasion when he would phone me before 7am to say he wanted to see me in his office in an hour's time. I knew I had either said or done something wrong or something that he was not happy with. But in all that happened whether good or challenging, I thank God for him. I thank him for his willingness to take me on in the first place, his willingness to allow me to preach on occasions, to release me when anything concerning Youth Alive was happening, and to let me run the youth and children's department as I wanted. I wish to greatly honour Pastor

Weaver, he was an excellent pastor, and his Bible teaching was second to none. Everyone knew that he was the boss. Pastor Weaver was not only the Senior Minister, but he, along with his wife, Dora, were also part of the cleaning team. He was the odd job man, if anything wanted doing, Pastor Weaver would be there to do it. Climbing ladders to clean out the guttering; laying a new floor in the minor hall; cleaning windows, whatever needed attention. Pastor Weaver wasn't above getting his hands dirty. However, it would be very rare if you saw Pastor Weaver in casual attire, as whatever he was doing, preaching or cleaning windows he would always have a shirt and tie on.

He had seen Calvary Temple grow, he had the vision and the discernment to know that when the building where they used to worship on Samson Road, Sparkbrook, had become too small and that the church needed to move to a bigger building. This decision was confirmed when on one Bonfire Night the church was burnt to the ground; it's thought that someone threw a firework through the letter box. Pastor Weaver and the leadership found an empty old Methodist building in Balsall Heath so the leadership, by faith, bought this church. It was badly run down and needed a lot of work doing. However, through Pastor Weaver's practical skills he managed to renovate and transform the building.

I did not take it for granted that I would be the next Senior Minister of Calvary Temple, but when the opportunity arose I applied for the job as I believed that God wanted me to take the next step. On the day of the vote one of the church elders, John Walton, called me around midnight and told me that I had got the post, but it was not a unanimous decision, as some of the deacons had not voted for me. One deacon told me the following Sunday that as soon as Pastor Weaver had gone, he and his family and friends would also be leaving the church. The week after Pastor Weaver left the church about 30 people also left. This deacon had been true to his word and along with family and friends he left. Not a brilliant start to me being the Senior Minister.

My own induction service took place the week after Pastor Weaver left. It was a great honour to have Warwick preach that day. I discovered in my new role that being the Senior Minister was not at all 'easy' in fact it was the opposite. It was, at times, very hard. I strongly believe that to be a Senior Minister, you need to have no doubts at all that the call of God to go into the ministry is upon you. People think that the Minister should be all things to all men. That is impossible. You cannot please all the people all of the time. People think that Ministers of churches only work one day a week – if only! Knowing the call of God upon your life is of great importance. You may have written a great sermon, or be asked to lead 'worship', or spoken at some debate, but unless your words are blessed of God, and you are full of the Holy Spirit, all that is produced or said are mere words, and won't do a lot of good. Prayer greatly helps you to speak with the power of the Holy Spirit upon you, and then you will see people respond to what you are saying, and it will help to shape their lives. The step up from being the Youth and Children's pastor was a very big step indeed. I was expected to be on hand for any problems, answer questions, give instructions and wise counsel. I had to undertake hospital visits, funerals, weddings, baptisms, counselling and so on, plus prepare for the Sunday sermons. This was a whole new experience for me!

When I became the senior minister, I soon realised that I would be doing a lot more preaching.

My good friend Alan Hewitt greatly helped me to do this. He would send me all the messages that he had preached and was preaching in his local church. He was a great preacher. The tapes would come with the understanding that I could use any of the materials from his studies. These tapes were indeed a 'God send' to me and brought great blessing to the church. Being the senior minister was quite daunting. I remember that first week after I had been inducted at the Senior Minister going to the back of the church after my first morning meeting. I was still awestruck realising that this was the beginning of a new season. As people left many wished me well in my new role saying that they would pray for me and that I had led the meeting well on my first morning. I felt much better after hearing their comments, however I was also overwhelmed that I was now responsible for their lives in regard to their walk with God. The fact hit me strongly! It was a very different feeling than the weeks before when someone else was in-charge, any big problems someone else would sort them out, but now it was my role! Thank

God, I had such a great leadership team on hand to help give me wisdom, guidance and supported me in prayer.

To bring vision and a plan to move the church forward was challenging, that's why I am grateful that I had such a strong leadership team who would offer me support. They may not have always fully agreed with what I wanted to do but they were always with me. It is so true that you can only bring people up to the level that you are yourself in God. It is also true that you cannot please everyone who is part of the church, that is why some people come and some people go. I thank God for the men and woman of God who were part of the leadership at Calvary Temple. People like John Walton, Eric Beardmore, Richard Davis, Vincent Ricketts, Simon Lakin, Bradford Ricketts, Vernon Dore, Sharon Davis (Mullin) and Pauline Bates. Another man of God, but who was not part of our leadership team was Billy Richards. It was very rare for him not to have a smile on his face; he was always loud, good to be with, and a great encouragement to me.

At the start of my career as Senior Minister it was overwhelming and extremely hard. Sometimes I made the wrong decisions, but that's why you need God to be close to you. With the anointing of the Holy Spirit upon you, you can always come through. I have made many mistakes in my life, too many to number, but here's the good news, God does not write people off because mistakes have been made. It reminds me of a story in the Bible. It starts where David the shepherd boy comes on the scene, and sometime after he had killed Goliath, he became the best King that Israel had ever had. But he made massive mistakes, he was a failure in many ways, yet God called him a Man after God's own heart. I am so glad that God is able to look past our mistakes, and looks at the intent of the heart. God can look past those mistakes if we say we are sorry and God does not just look past our mistakes, he forgets them. How amazing is that! God does not want my life or yours to be de¬railed in any way, but when we focus on past failures it will hinder our ability to move on.

One of the first things we did when I became the Senior Minister was to change the name of the church; it was called 'Calvary Temple'. We felt that because we were surrounded with many temples, it would be good to change the name, so that people walking past would know who we were.

We asked the church people to suggest names and then vote. 'Kings Christian Centre' came out on top. I wish that I had kept the paper on which all the potential names for the church were written, there were some weird and wonderful names, one was 'Noah's Ark'.

Kings Christian Centre, Birmingham

When I first arrived in Birmingham, most of the church people lived in Balsall Heath. Quite a few lived on the street where the church was. It was mainly West Indian people who lived there alongside a few white people. Over the years that has changed dramatically, as now around 99% of the community is Asian. We had a factory opposite the church, but today there is a large mosque. Once parking was easy, but today it is a nightmare to park your car.

Because the youth and children's work was so strong numerically and spiritually, the leadership wanted to appoint a Youth Pastor, it would be a paid full¬-time post. I remember advertising the post and, as a result we interviewed a few people and asked them to do something at a youth meeting to assess their capabilities. We appointed a young man by the name of Lukas Dewhirst whose father was the Senior Minister at the East Ham Assemblies of God Church.

Lukas and I knew each other quite well because he'd attended youth camps in Great Walstead. He was a fine Godly young man. It was an excellent appointment, everyone loved Lukas, and he soon got involved in all aspects of the church. The youth thought he was great. Lukas stayed for four years, so when he decided to go to a Bible College to study more, we were very upset, we did not want to lose him.

Advertising for the next youth pastor threw up a surprise as somehow a young couple got to hear of this vacancy in Canada. This was Phil and Christina Smith, who we appointed youth pastors. They did a great job while they were with us. They could get a mortgage for a lovely house, but unfortunately Christina felt homesick, so after being with us for just a year, they decided to return to Canada. So, my third youth pastor in 5 years was sought out.

We appointed Aaron Partington. He had the call of God on his life which was apparent from a young age. We knew Aaron very well before he came to Birmingham because our two families went on holiday every year. Our two boys got on famously with Aaron and they have their own stories to tell. Aaron loved God with all his heart and like his dad, was full of fun and mischief. It was great to be in his company. Just as Lukas did a great job working as the Youth and Children's pastor, similarly so did Aaron. Everybody loved him (especially the girls) and I can still recall them both leading and preaching in church. Whilst in Birmingham, Aaron stayed at our house, so for a few years it was great to have Simon, Daniel and Aaron in the home.

There was so much fun happening at home, so much laughter and noise. It was great to see these three lads enjoying life. We were very sorry when Aaron left us, the whole church was upset. But it's great to know that both Lukas and Aaron are in the ministry right now, they both lead their respective churches, one in Warrington, and the other in the Liverpool area. To have had these two young men as my youth pastors were indeed great years. I am highly delighted that I have been privileged to share in their lives and played a small part in their development as leaders. I commend the then leadership of Kings Christian Centre, who like me saw that boys and girls are the church of today and decided that employing a youth pastor was indeed the right decision. If you want to keep young people today in church, then look for a young man or woman to lead your youth (if possible pay them to be full-time).

The young people who were around in Lukas and Aaron's time will tell you that their appointment was a God appointment. I can see still today, Lukas and Aaron leading Sunday morning worship, driving around collecting the kids and young people to bring to church, spending time with the elderly, organising days out with the youngsters, seeking God to bring the word of the Lord, having loads of fun, making serving Jesus such an exciting thing to do.

I thank God for both.

CHAPTER 12

CHILDREN AND YOUTH CAMPS

lthough I was Senior Minister I still felt that my calling for children's work had never left me, and I still believed (and continue to) that camps are a great opportunity and experience for young people. During the time Lukas was with us, I remember getting a telephone call from Ian Green, who used to be the National Youth Alive Team Leader. He told me of a school that wanted to open their premises in the summer to groups of children or young people. Would I be interested?

I was, so Lukas and I made the journey to visit Howell's School in North Wales to check out their facilities.

We met with the bursar of the school who showed us around, as we were keen to know if the facilities were good enough. It was an excellent girl's boarding school, with four accommodation blocks comprising of 350 beds, an open-air swimming pool, a large gym, eight tennis courts and lots of fields to run around and play games in.

Compared to Great Walstead, this was by far a much better venue. It was during the month of March that we travelled down to the school. We asked the bursar if there were any weeks available in either July or August and we could book two weeks. I don't remember what the numbers were like for our two weeks of youth camp, but they went down a storm.

Howell's School, Wales

A lot of good came about during those two weeks, people becoming Christians, those who were cold towards the things of God began to start following Jesus again. Those two weeks were the start of many years, which still continue today, of having great camps for both young people and boys and girls at venues across the country. My wife Lesley, does a great deal of the work, booking everyone in, arranging the food and menus and generally making sure that everyone is well fed.

One day we received notice that we could not use Howell's School one year; it was around March time that we heard. Bookings were already coming in for camp, both youth and children so to have this news so late in the day was not good, we were gutted. Some organisation wanted to use the school for all of the six weeks' summer holiday, so we were told that our weeks were cancelled. We contacted a solicitor to see if he would help us in the matter. He sent a letter to the school to remind them that we had signed a contract to use their premises. Happily, Robbie Locke, who oversaw the school, invited Lukas and I to meet him. As a result, we could have access to every area of school. So, we got the four blocks of accommodation, plus the headmaster's house and the kitchen area etc. I need to thank Robbie for all his great help over many years.

One year however, we were not able to hire the school, so Lukas, Tony Williams, and I went all around the country looking at other schools to use. Some down south were really good, but the cost was far too much. We heard about an organisation not too far away from Howell's called Colomendy; we went to see the place. It was a bit run down and the accommodation was not great but it had beds for around 350 people. Lukas and I decided to go for it and we spent the next four years at Colomendy.

One of the accommodation blocks was just like an army camp, one big room with about 40 beds in it and one toilet in the middle of the room. We had to do three sittings for every meal, which was time consuming. They had a very tiny indoor swimming pool, but they had some very good activities such as zip wires and caving that were based in the forest nearby. We held our meetings in a marquee. On our fourth visit, we saw a remarkable change at Colomendy. Since our previous visit the place had had a 'face lift'. Gone were the army barracks, instead you had en¬-suite rooms, one bed in each room. The activities were really good; in the nearby forest they had created climbing walls, a giant zip wire and an obstacle course. After those four years, we were invited back to Howell's to run both youth camps and children's camps. We felt that it would be good to ask some others to run the youth camps, but we would still run our children's camp for one week instead of two.

Youth camp at Howell's school

CHAPTER 13

HAPPY HOLIDAYS

We first started going on holiday with John and Andrene Partington when they were pastoring in the Isle of Wight, we went there for two years. It was the start of having lots of holidays with the Partington family. If you know John well, you will know that our holidays were great, so much fun was had and there was always the 'unexpected' which John would no doubt had instigated.

We went to places such as Devon, Cornwall, Center Parcs, we even went on a cruise for 10 days. For one holiday, we asked Pastor Fred Weaver if we could use his car. I can't recall why we didn't use our own cars, but when we arrived, our apartment was on the second floor of the apartment block. So John decided that to save us carrying our luggage up those flights of stairs, he would stand on the roof of Pastor Weaver's car and hand the luggage up to me on the second floor. When John stepped off the roof we noticed a big dent! To say Pastor Weaver was not a happy man, was an understatement, we never dare ask him again.

Aaron, Daniel, Simon, Heidi and John

I remember that I had booked a week's holiday at Center Parcs in Sherwood Forest for all of us. We arrived on the Saturday only to find that most of the bikes that you hire had gone and there was no queue at reception, in fact it was very quiet around that area. But the following Friday, we saw everyone taking back their bikes, we made enquiries as to why they were they leaving on the Friday only to be told that the booking was from Friday to Friday. You can imagine the comments thrown my way for getting it wrong! We went back the following year, Friday to Friday.

Besides John and I being great friends, we would also look forward to seeing each other. While he was the Senior Minister at Bedworth Church we saw quite a lot of each other. Even though John loved to have a laugh, when you needed help, encouragement and a pick-me-up, John was always on hand.

CHAPTER 14

FINDING A NEW HOME

The area around the church was changing fast; many of those who attended the church who lived in Balsall Heath were moving out and going to live in other areas of the city. The factory across from the church had closed and instead of the parking becoming better, it became a nightmare. A decision was taken by the oversight team to look around to see if there were any buildings that we could purchase where access to the church was easier. We found one or two properties that could be our answer. We went to see a plot of land that had a big garage complex on it in Hall Green. It had a room that could seat around 200 people, smaller rooms that could house our youth and kid's ministry, and lots of people passing the property every day. Best of all it had a car park to the rear of the building that would hold 50 cars. There was one down side. It had an asbestos roof and was in need of repair.

We also went to see a church that had closed down in Moseley that also seated over 200 people but the main hall was long and not very wide. It had a minor hall and quite a bit of parking. We were very interested in this property, and on a couple of Sundays, we had our church services there. We even had the church surveyed but the report came back that the church walls were crumbling on the outside and would need a few thousand pounds to repair.

I went to see a Jewish synagogue also in Moseley, but although it was quite big, it was not big enough to accommodate us. We saw a few more properties, but none of them were suitable. Then one day an old cinema in Small Heath came on to the market, with an asking price of £300,000. It seated 1,200 people – 800 downstairs and 400 upstairs.

The seating downstairs had been taken out, but the upstairs was intact. The stage was very big, with rooms behind it. On the very top floor were also rooms, the main one being the projector room; from there you could see the neighbouring Birmingham City football ground. It was situated on the A45 – one of the main roads from

Birmingham to Coventry. It could also accommodate about 50 cars. Behind it was a decent housing estate, and on the opposite side of the cinema was a McDonalds. I remember taking the leadership team and their partners to have a look around the building.

Then, Margaret Walton (an elder's wife) told us about a dream she had which was all about what building we ought to be looking at and should buy. This old cinema in Small Heath was just like the building in her dream. We were over the moon. It had everything we needed and more. We put in an offer at the asking price, only to be told that someone had already bought the property, a housing company. To say we were devastated was an understatement. I remember telling the congregation the following Sunday morning that we had lost the building. Then Louison Ricketts (another elder's wife) stood up and prophesied to the whole church saying that we were not to give up hope because the building would come back on the market.

True enough, some ten months later, I had a call saying the cinema was back on the market and we had first refusal.

We were overjoyed. God had come through for us. The prophesy had come to pass. We decided to bring the whole congregation to the building to have a look around, everyone was so excited. The potential was immense.

We organised a building project team to make plans for the building. We employed Peter Cumberlack to be the project manager and chairman of the building team to help us fulfil our dream. We knew when we had bought the place that there was asbestos in the roof of the building; this did not concern us as we were going to re-furbish the cinema and only paint the asbestos ceiling.

So, we drew up some building plans and submitted them to the council for their approval. But when we heard from the council we were again devastated, they had said that the building was old and an eyesore to passers-by, and the only thing we could do if we wanted our church on this land was to pull it down and begin again. We had spent a lot of money getting our plans ready, we had met with a few small grant giving trusts to see if they would help us; we'd even approached Kingdom Bank (part of Assemblies of God) for a loan. After many meetings with Kingdom

Bank we finally got our mortgage.

A big problem was because the building had to come down, we knew straight away that the asbestos would now be a massive problem to us. We asked for a few quotes from companies that specialised in removing asbestos and the cheapest cost to pull down the building came to £110,000. But a cost we felt willing to pay.

I remember watching as the building was knocked down. I was so sad. All we had at the end of this act was an acre of flat land. We started to fundraise again but on a bigger scale. We needed to get new plans drawn up, pray and believe that as God had got the land for us, then God would be with us in this new venture. One very good thing that came out of all this was that the land was made into a car park for the Birmingham City Football Club games. With a full car park, we were taking nearly £1,000 per game, so each year we would take around £20,000. Birmingham City was then in the premiership, so the car park was full each time.

My sincere thanks go out to people like Gerald, Bradford, Lyndon, Denzil, Zephaniah, Len, Lewis and others, who would spend hours helping at the car park at every home game. And today, years later some of these lads, Gerald, Bradford, Denzil and Lyndon are still down at the car park, helping us. Thanks guys! That is really serving Jesus, their commitment is second to none, there's no shelter when it rains, no fire when it's cold, but sheer dedication in doing what they can for the kingdom.   I salute these guys.

By this time, our project manager had gone and instead we had two young men from London drawing up plans and meeting with the council people, trying to raise funds for us. Yvette John had also joined us full time as the project manager. Yvette worked extremely hard for us, getting local people interested in coming to the church in Ombersley Road for activities. This was amazing because by now all the people who lived in Balsall Heath were mainly Asian and from very different cultures, so for an Asian lady to come into a Christian church was unexpected.   Thanks Yvette for all your hard work, you did a great job. God will reward you.

I remember going by train to London with Yvette and John Walton to see these two young men and see how our project was going. We thought we had a deal with Advantage West Midland and Future Builders. Plans had been passed by the city council so we were in a good position to start the building. But at our next meeting with Advantage West Midlands the news was given that the offer to help was being withdrawn. This was the third time we were devastated in our quest to see the building go up. The congregation had put thousands of pounds into the building project, and once again the door had been shut. But we believed that God's timing is always correct, so we awaited God's timing. As I write, planning permission to build on that land has been agreed and the church is planned to begin construction in 2017. A 20-year dream is now being fulfilled!

CHAPTER 15

PASSING ON THE BATON

For those who are in the 'ministry' today, please pray for them, they are on the front line, and believe me it's hard, very hard. The number of times I wrote out my resignation both in Pastor Weaver's days and when I was the man in charge was innumerable. What kept me going? It's what keeps every minister going, and everyone else who is serving Jesus – the call of God.

Many have said before, that church without people would be wonderful. As a Minister, you must take a lot on the chin and things that happen are not always other people's fault, sometimes they are our fault. That's why we need the gifts of the Holy Spirit, the gift of discernment, words of knowledge and wisdom.

As a Minister, I did not always get it right, but that's why I needed Godly men and women on my leadership team. There have been times when I have gone home, broken-hearted. On the other hand, I am delighted when people feel the call God to go into the ministry, to be a missionary, or go and work within another Christian organisation.

There is a danger that in our walk with God, our journey could make us become people of information rather than people of action. We know what the Bible says about any situation we find ourselves in, but do we take the action that it gives? We can talk a good fight rather than fight a good fight. We sometimes confuse knowledge with active faith. Knowledge is not enough we need a revelation of what we know. Information about the Bible will not do us much good, but a revelation of the Jesus will change our lives. God says come to me through Jesus and your past will be forgiven. That sounds great and it is great if you believe it. Yet, so many fear the past, scared that it might come to light. You need to believe, come to faith and as far as God is concerned the past is past, wiped clean.

There are 'seasons' in all of our lives, and after being in Calvary Temple / Kings Christian Centre for 35 years I began to feel that it was time to look for my successor. Even though things were going well in the church, people being saved, people growing in God, the building project was still in my heart, the youth and kids work going well, silver liners being looked after well, I felt it was time to hand over the baton. And, if my season at Kings was coming to an end I wanted the transition to be a God transition. I knew that in Assemblies of God there weren't many good change-overs, so I was determined that the appointment would be a 'God appointment'. I decided that I would only tell my elders, and see what happened.

A few months later an email landed on my desk from the other side of the world – Australia. It was from a guy called Kirk McAtear, who was an Assembly of God Minister looking for a move to England. He felt the call of God to come to the UK. I was amazed at what he had put in his email. He said that he had heard that I was looking to vacate my post!

That got me thinking, has he had a word of knowledge? How does he know that information? Then I remembered an Australian coming through the church who had made an appointment to see me. He wanted King's Christian Centre to be one of his satellite churches in the UK. I was not at all interested in him doing that, but in our conversation, I must have mentioned about me looking for my successor. Anyway, the Bible says that God moves in mysterious ways, and it seemed a potential successor was coming from overseas!

Unbeknownst to me, months previously Kirk was in a church in Australia when this guy who had been to see me, sat next to him. They did not know each other. He asked Kirk where he was ministering and during that conversation Kirk mentioned about the call of God to go to the UK but he had no contacts there, so this guy mentioned my name. Was this the 'God Appointment' that I was hoping for?

I emailed back and said to Kirk, you may come, but you will need to pay for your own flight and to book a hotel in Birmingham. You will not be asked to preach, but you are still welcome to come. I wanted to make this visit as hard as I could, so that if Kirk was my successor, he would still come even if he had to pay his own way. Kirk emailed me back to say that he would come.

I remember picking him up in Manchester. As we got in

the car to come home, I knew in my spirit that this was God's man for the church. We seemed to get on very well as we set off back home and the conversation all the way was good, positive and interesting. It was a Friday evening and we arrived just in time to pop into the church and to see the boys and girls having their meeting. Afterwards we went upstairs to see how the young people were doing. With all the leaders, youth and children, Kirk seemed very much to be enjoying himself, chatting away to everyone and quite at home.

As I dropped him off at his hotel, I mentioned that the next day I was going to a thanksgiving service of the brother of Nick McDavid who had died. This was to be held at a church that was opposite Howell's School in North Wales, and would he like to come with me? He said yes, so we went together. I had a strong feeling in my spirit that Kirk was the man to take over the church.

He told me about his family, how Tracee, his wife, also felt the call of God to the UK, and their two children were fine about coming too. On our way back to Birmingham, I asked him if he would like to speak in the Sunday morning service, to which he said that he would love to.

Kirk is a very positive man, full of the life of God, his preaching was very good and he seemed to mingle well with everyone, it was as if King's was his church already. He was extremely friendly, great company to be around, and it seemed that everyone took to him immediately. He stayed a few days. The leadership team met and it was decided unanimously that we ought to invite him to come again and bring his wife with him, and this time we would pay.

Kirk and Tracee arrived a few months later and stayed with us for around 10 days. Again, the church leadership met and after some talk it was agreed by all that Kirk and Tracee were this 'God appointment' that we were all praying for. To find and appoint your successor is not only very important, but difficult and scary too. I believed that God had sent this family, but after being in the Church for 35 years, it was extremely hard to pass the baton on to someone else. Nevertheless, the building of God's church is more important than my worries of 'what do I do next?'

So, next on the agenda was the arrival of the whole

McAtear family. So, it was good to meet Kirk and Tracee's two children, Josiah and Ruby. How they must have felt I do not know, but it must have been very hard and difficult for them too. The leadership agreed that for the next three months Kirk and I would work together, with myself being still the Senior Minister. Those three months went very quickly, soon it would be time to leave King's Christian Centre, but knowing that the right people were in charge brought great comfort to Lesley and me.

The McAtear family

Simon and Daniel, my sons, had arranged a surprise event to celebrate Lesley and I being at Kings for 35 years. We knew nothing about this. We thought there would be just a 'leaving event' on a Sunday. We had invited our good friends John and Andrene Partington to speak on that Sunday. They arrived the day before and John said that he was going to take us out for a meal. We went into town and parked near to a big restaurant, went inside, ordered a drink, then after a while John said, we won't stay here, so back in the car we got and drove away. As John drove I thought something was up, but John often did crazy, spur of the moment things. But we were now travelling towards church.

As we arrived at the church, Bradford, a deacon came running out to remove some bollards so as to get John's car in. We then went to the side entrance and into the church. The main church was in darkness, but that's where we were heading. Suddenly the lights of the main hall were switched on, and the loud cry of 'surprise' went up. The place was packed, not just with the people that came to church, but many of Lesley and my friends. As we sat on the front row, Aaron Partington came from the minor hall with a big red book in his hand. He turned to us, welcomed us and then began a two hour 'This Is Your Life' event which had been put together.

It was good to see so many people. Lots of things took place that night, we sang kids songs with all the actions. We heard via video link from Roger Blackmore from Long Island in the U.S.A., and from John King who was living in Chicago. Lukas was there too. It was a wonderful surprise to see so many familiar faces. The next day was our official leaving day; it was good to have John Partington as the speaker. I remember passing on a physical baton in the service to Kirk and Tracee. I have to say, that was one of the hardest things I have ever done in my life – passing on that baton. King's had been my life for the past 35 years, 16 of those as the Youth and Children's Minister and 19 years as the Senior Minister. I left that day hoping but also believing that God had something still for me to do.

Three generations of church leaders: Kirk McAtear, Fred Weaver and Dave

CHAPTER 16

FRESH START- AGAIN

To give Kirk room to establish himself as Senior Minister myself and Lesley believed the best thing to do would be to leave the church. This would not only help Kirk have the freedom and confidence to step into his role, but would also avoid confusion for the congregation. We did know occasions when some Senior Ministers had stepped down and stayed in the same church. We understand why they did that as they had built their life in their church and after retiring did not want to leave their friends and family. Both myself and Lesley knew it would be incredibly difficult to leave Kings as it had been such a part of our lives. Our family served there, our life-long friends were there. However, we felt strongly that for a good transition to take place, we needed to be out of the way.

Having left King's, Lesley and I wondered where we could go. It didn't feel right to go to a different Birmingham church, so we had a dilemma – where do we go on Sundays? My good friend Tony Williams, who was an elder at Christian Life Ministries in Coventry, suggested that we could go there on Sundays.

Tony and I have been friends for years, so even though the journey was around 45 minutes to get from Birmingham to Coventry, we decided to go the following Sunday. Tony was at the door waiting for us and he took us to some seats near the front where Julie, his wife, was seated. At the end of the service, Senior Minister, Mick Bonner welcomed us and asked us to come to the front so that he and the elders could pray for us.

He gave the impression that we would be making C.L.M. our spiritual home. I knew John Froggett and Dave Bolton as they were the main leaders in the kid's and youth ministry, we had met on a few occasions at the Ultimate Youth and Children's Camp that I had been running at Howells School in North Wales for many years, and when I had come over to Coventry to talk to either the youth or children; but I didn't know many others.

Lesley and I decided that although it was a long journey

we would make C.L.M. our spiritual home. The first Sunday we went to C.L.M. they showed a video of their new building project. I knew all about this because the company that was to build their new building was introduced by me, as they were the ones who were going to build our new church in Birmingham. As I watched the video I must admit I was very sad, because I thought it should have been the new King's Christian Centre that should be being built. The project was huge, much, much bigger than King's was to be, with the main auditorium seating around 650 people.

After being there a few months I was asked by the Leadership Team of Coventry if I would consider working for the church three days each week. This was a 'God appointment' for me. I did not and still don't think that my time involved in the work of God had come to an end. If you retire from the Ministry at 65, then what you have been doing was just a job for you; the call of God is still on your life until the day you die. So, when Mick Bonner kindly asked if I would do an audit of the church, to go into every department and look at the strength and weaknesses, and suggest ways of improving things, I was over the moon. I felt that to ask me to look into the 'health of the church' was amazing. We did not know each other well, but he was still very willing to see how things could improve within the church and was not fazed by any of the reports that I presented him with.

Mick was an incredibly discerning man, and confident in his call. He knew that someone looking at the local church with different eyes, outside eyes, would see much more than those inside the church. In asking for this to be done, I felt that Mick was a great man of God who was open to change, and not afraid of another minister looking at the church where he was the Senior Pastor. Remarkable considering so many could feel intimidated, however Mick wanted to use my years of expertise and wisdom. I was honoured that he put so much trust in me.

I was asked to do two things; number one was to meet up with all the elders, their wives, heads of department and teams of every department in the church. This I did, I met with all the above on a one-to-one basis, and there were about 70 leaders. Without a doubt, this was the most interesting, exciting, productive and rewarding thing that I ever did in C.L.M.

Number two; mentoring. This does not seem to happen in many churches, but to me it's vital to get someone to mentor your leaders/workers. It shows them that you are interested in them, grateful for the ministry that they do. You want to encourage them as much as possible, and help them develop their ministry.

During the four years I was doing that, I met these leaders and teams on a one to one basis on numerous occasions and spent lots of time together with them either at church or in their own homes. On a few occasions, I would meet up with some of the lads at the local golf driving range.

I believe that mentoring these good people was also a 'God send' for them too. I pray that I helped them to make better decisions; get closer to God and helped them to know which 'ministry' God had called them to, and how to be most effective.

I remember going to meet up with a family, who did not come to church very often. When I met them at the door of their home, the man said to me: "You coming today to see us has saved our lives." They were on the verge of leaving church, they felt no part of it; their two daughters had lost interest and their walk with God was almost non-existent. Today, thank the Lord; they are still in the church, going on well for God.

It was also my privilege to go to many homes and meet people who were part of C.L.M. They were not leaders or part of any team, but C.L.M. was their spiritual home. I have concluded that most people who come to church would love someone to take an interest in them and their children. To just sit down with them, have a coffee together and chat. In my experience that is what people want – to feel part of their local church, to have confidence in sharing troubles with someone, and discovering how to know God better. If these kinds of things aren't done, then all you have on Sundays is a crowd; with a few being part of your 'core' group.

On a few occasions, we would all meet and look at ways of being a better leader. How to work at being a 'team' and how seeking God in prayer and Bible reading was vital to their success.

The time was getting nearer to seeing the plans passed by

the city council for the church building project. Again, I was asked by the leadership if I would help in getting some finance to help to build the new church. So we formed a 'fund raising team' to look at ways of doing that. The team were great, worked very hard, came up with some big ideas, and overall our fund raising was a great success. We did the 'normal' stuff like sponsored walks and car boot sales. We also did 'buy a chair, sofa and building fund', plus offerings three times a year, as well as preaching on tithing. The response from the congregation was great, they turned up at all the fundraising events, volunteering to help in any way they could, filled in gift aid forms, started to tithe – all brilliant stuff.

From a very early age I was taught the principal of tithing, to give God what was rightfully His – 10% of what I earned. I started to practice this from around 12 years of age. Sometimes I thought 'I cannot afford to do this,' but I did it because I couldn't afford not to tithe.

Over the years, God has been true to his word, I have witnessed the promises of God come to pass many times. Today I have a large detached house overlooking a golf course and the mortgage all paid for. We have never lacked for anything. Dear Reader, God has been so good to us. If you are not tithing to the local church and it's your 'home' church, may I encourage you to start today. You will never lack for anything as God always honours those who honour Him.

On the day of the church opening, everyone, congregation and visitors alike were amazed at what they saw. The building was awesome. The construction company did us proud. As far as I know there isn't another church in AoG like this one in Coventry. One of the main men building the new church was Richard Williams. Richard attended C.L.M. along with his wife and family. He went for an interview with Provision and got one of the main jobs. The Williams family are a great family to have in the church, they all love God and between them they possess great gifts of leadership, all of them have a servant heart, very balanced in their lifestyle. Now in charge of the youth work in church and doing a great job. I prophesy that their son, Luke will one day be a great leader, someone who will make a massive difference to many people, someone who already has the anointing of God upon his life.

On that opening day, it was good to see Jeff Pickup, who had been invited to be the main speaker at the opening. John and Andrene Partington were also with the main party. We had hired a gospel choir from Birmingham to sing, and we had a Coventry band playing in the car park. The place was packed; we had around 650 people present. Pastor Mick Bonner must have been over the moon with what he saw; his dream had come to pass, and no doubt in his mind it was much, much better than he had ever hoped for. Pastor Mick is a Godly man, although a very quiet man, he was loved by everyone. He was a man of prayer, there were times when I went to see him in his office and he would be on his knees praying. He was a great pastor. One of the things that this newly built church did was to see a big influx of people coming to the church. They were mainly of African descent. Some did not stay, but some are still in the church today. It is true that the African people bring 'life' to the house of God, and are very friendly.

Another of my highlights of being in C.L.M. was sharing an office with a few people such as Dave Bolton, Alex Hart and Jamie Crosby. No doubt about it, besides working hard, we had some great fun, they would often 'hijack' my phone and computer and put their faces on; or would turn my desk around, so I was facing the wall. But these three young men are highly skilled and gifted in what they do. Alex is an outstanding young man, who loves God and has a great gift in music and kids work. He has produced kid's worship songs, organised and ran a 'get on the stage' ministry, managed to get into a couple of schools, and is the leader of Rangers, which is a mid- week, high energy kids programme. He has the makings of being a Youth and Children's Pastor one day. I highly recommend him.

Mick Bonner was due to retire six months after the new church was built, however in order to give a new person an opportunity to take the new building from day one, he decided he would step down earlier than planned. Wow! I found that to be truly amazing, what a gracious step that was. The fact that Mick had spent many hours working on this building, it had been his vision, and, through obedience to God, to decided step down so that he did not even preach in the new building that he had been so passionately involved in seeing built, is just evidence of what a humbling, obedient person he was.

At the beginning of 2012, Martin and Esther Storey were appointed as Senior Ministers at C.L.M. No doubt about it, it was another 'God appointment'. They had come from David Shearman's church in Nottingham. They are doing a great job; God is blessing their ministry. There are now many more people attending C.L.M. than at any time in its history.

Jon Froggett, who had been the Assistant Pastor to Mick also left. He and Jo had done a great job at C.L.M. but an excellent opportunity had come his way, and he is now the Senior Minister at Rugby. Alongside his wife, Jo, they make a great team. Again, another 'God appointment'. Dave Bolton, the Youth Pastor also left and gone to take over the church at Leamington Spa. Yet again, a 'God appointment'. Concerning Jon Froggett and Dave Bolton, you could not wish for anything other than good for these two men. It must have been very hard to have left the church they had poured endless energy into after being there such a decent amount of time and playing such an important role in the church. As they saw the building being built, they must have thought that they would play a major role in the new church. But it wasn't to be, but I strongly believe that right now they are where God wants them to be.

CHAPTER 17

ANNUS HORRIBILIS

2013 was a very difficult year for me and I was glad to see the back of it. I remember the Queen giving her speech one Christmas Day, and she described that year as an 'Annus Horribilis' year. Lots of things had happened within the Royal Family, so much so that the Queen said that she was glad when that year was over. 2013 was an 'Annus Horribilis' year for me too.

For many years I'd had difficulties with my feet and my knees. My doctor said it was because I played too much sport when growing up. My feet have osteoarthritis and my knees are bad because the cartilage is gone and the bones are now rubbing together. I had been going to the hospital for a few years to have injections in both knees. But now the right knee was so bad an operation was the only way forward. So, in April 2013 I went into hospital to be operated on. I was home within three days but off work for quite some time, and unable to drive for six weeks – so no golf! This was incredibly hard, I didn't realise how I need to be around so many people, socialising is important for me and not being able to get out and about really affected my mood. I still find it difficult to kneel on my right knee.

Then in the August I developed bladder trouble, causing me so much pain I ended up in A & E. This all happened three days before I was due to run a week of camp in North Wales. I was in so much pain during the week, I was just glad that Lukas was there as I could do very little, and really, I only wanted to go home. Back home I found that I would have to wait at least six weeks for a hospital appointment, so I made the decision to go private. Another operation but then a loss of blood resulted in me having a blood transfusion.

Back home I was still feeling very ill and now also suffering from anaemia. I was told to eat spinach and liver and drink a can of Guinness every day. A can of Guinness! I am tee-total but had to drink a can of Guinness every day. Both sons found this very funny and often teased me about acting like a drunkard. These days I feel much better, but I had lost a lot of time regarding work and if I'm honest I struggled to pick up the pace again.

The Bible is a wonderful book, full of the promises of God. Throughout history many have tried to destroy or completely remove the Bible so that no one could even get a copy. My favourite promise is found in Romans chapter 8 verse 28 . . . for we know that all things work together for good, to them that love God. It's that word all that gets my attention. Not some things, but all things work together for good in my life.

For as long as I can remember, Romans chapter 8 verse 28 has always been my favourite verse in the Bible, and I do strongly believe what it says, that all things in our life work out for good. But during 2013 I was wondering if God had forgotten all about me and the promise He had made, because I could not see any good things happening in my life.

My daily devotions were greatly affected, I was feeling down and depressed. I found that when things were good in my life, Romans chapter 8 verse 28 did not come into my mind. It's hard sometimes just to trust God, I knew in my heart that the words in Romans are the Word of the

Lord, but it is not easy to believe that when things are not good in your life. For everyone there are 'seasons', my times at the print shop; my time travelling the country; my time at the shoe shop; my time in Birmingham; my time at Coventry, were all seasons in my life. Looking back these health issues were just a season, but I found it quite difficult at times to deal with.

Once I recovered I returned to work at C.L.M church, but it turned out that it would only be for three more months as my contract was not the be renewed. Being part of C.L.M. for the past four years was good for me, but now I had to trust that God had something new for me to do. I had to believe that God brings out the good in every situation.

It was great working alongside Mick, Jon and Dave and of course the church elders. I was really looked after well and am extremely grateful for them allowing me to do what I did.

Perhaps things have happened in your life which have caused you to say: 'Where's the good in that?' Life throws all kinds of things at you, bad things as well as good things. Sometimes I have asked this question: 'Why God?

What's the purpose in this?' Some things that have happened I have not understood. Maybe you are going through a tough time. Something has happened which you can't understand and the question – 'Why God?' has come out of your mouth.

My comment would always be: 'Trust in the Lord with all of your heart, don't lean towards your own understanding, but in all your ways acknowledge Him and He will direct your paths'. Proverbs chapter 3 verse 5-6.

CHAPTER 18

A NEW SEASON OF MY LIFE

So, after leaving Christian Life Ministries I had no idea what I was going to do. Lesley and I had met with Kirk and Tracee regarding the possibility of us going back to Kings, now renamed Connect Church, but not to take on a role as such. They kindly agreed that it would be fine with them, so we started to attend Connect Church. Although that wasn't hard as we knew most of the people, not having a role as such, proved to be difficult.

As I write I have no idea what the next season of my life will bring, but I'm excited at the thought of where God will take me next and still enjoy serving God through organising the yearly kid's camps. I have my three grandchildren to look after, which is hard work, but they are great kids, so it's well worth doing that.

IS GOD PULLING MY STRINGS? Yes, I truly believe that God is doing just that and has done that throughout my life, there were times when I had no idea where my ministry was going but I had constant faith in the One who plans my steps. We can often want to go our own way, do our own thing, but life can only be good, when we allow God to direct our steps. This is what God says in in the book of Jeremiah chapter 9 verse 11. 'For I know the plans I have for you, declares the Lord, plans to prosper you and not to harm you, plans to give you hope and a future.'

Another favourite verse of mine is in Psalms chapter 37 verse 23 where it says, 'The steps of a good man are ordered by the Lord.'

I turned 70 years of age in 2016! I know I don't look it or feel it, but it's a fact of life, I am 70 years old! I was fine when I reached 50 years of age, happy to mention it to anyone, and when my 60th and 65th came around, again I was okay about telling people. But when I turned 70, I kept that under wraps until I realised these facts:

Three of the people who were running to do the hardest job in the world – that of being President of the USA in 2017 are around my age. Hilary Clinton was 69, Bernie Sanders turned 75 and Donald Trump was 70. Five of the eight current Supreme Court justices are all over 65 and three are over 75. Winston Churchill was re-elected as Prime Minister at the age of 76 and served until he was 81. Ronald Reagan served as President from age 70 to 78. Then at 76 he stood against the USSR in West Berlin and told Mikhail Gorbachev to: "Tear down this wall." I realised that getting old doesn't mean I must stop.

In the secular world retirement starts at 65, we need to ensure this does not translate into church life too. That even though there are people in the church that are over the age of 65 they haven't retired from God's work. Ask yourself, did Moses retire? Or Paul, or Peter, or John? Do military officers retire in the middle of a war? Most men don't die of old age, they die of retirement. Through retirement I have on occasions found that I have lost my purpose, I have on occasions had to battle with trying to find my worth. However, I still have a passion to serve! Although my season has changed, I know that there are still good years ahead of me and I am waiting on God to direct me on how to best serve His kingdom. I am still seeking and believing that He directs my steps! So, there's still life in the old dog – still got what it takes to be a blessing, I'm just waiting for the opportunities, and I'm still allowing God to pull the strings in my life. It states in Psalms chapter 92 verses 12-15: 'The righteous... still bear fruit in old age'. Why would God tell us that? Because he wants us to dream that. He wants us to pray for that. Make no mistake, the Bible believes in retirement – it's called Heaven.

I have really enjoyed writing my autobiography, you never know what you can do until you try, as I look back I can see how God has been directing my steps, although at times I have walked alone, gone my own way and done my own thing. But when I let God order my life, life is so much more rewarding, purposeful and fulfilling. They say to stay youthful, stay useful.

We don't often talk about or even mention that Jesus is coming back one day to take His church to Heaven, but when that happens or if I am no longer on planet earth, I look forward to hear God say to me . . . 'Dave, well done.'

CHAPTER 19

THOSE WHO HAVE INSPIRED ME

L ooking back I salute my mother and father and my Uncle John for having so much faith and forward thinking. My parents are no longer with us, likewise my Uncle John and Auntie Betty, but I thank God for them, their encouragement, faithfulness and willingness to mentor and coach me during my life.

We all need to be mentored; we all need someone to speak into our lives, to oversee us, to help us grow, to help us make good decisions. I thank God for the people who in my life have been my mentors and encouragers who have spoken into my life – some of what people have said has not always been pleasant to the ears, but it was needed.

Throughout my life there have been so many people who have inspired me, strengthened me, helped me and cheered me along the way. So in gratitude to them I would like to honour them.

My wife – Lesley

In 2014 we celebrated 40 years of married life. As the wife of a pastor, Lesley has done a brilliant job. She is a very gifted lady and can certainly preach better than me, and no doubt she is also a better counsellor than me too. With me working from 6am to 9pm, with just lunch and an evening meal in between, life was very difficult sometimes for her. When the boys arrived on the scene, it was even harder for Lesley. I was hardly at home, church life seemed to had taken over my life. I was always there, but had no choice in the matter, so my boys were in bed when I went out in a morning and in bed when I returned home at night most nights.

If I had another go, I would do life much differently. Yes,

God must always come first, but then family and finally church. Church life has not always been straightforward, being in the ministry has to be a God calling, otherwise you would not survive.

Throughout all of our 35 years in the Birmingham church, Lesley has been extremely supportive, she has not always agreed with what I want to do or have done, but has still backed me 100%. I cannot thank her enough.

Right now, Lesley loves being a grandmother to Summer, Eden and Mylah, and she is excellent at it. And she still serves in the local church. It must be in her blood!

My sons – Simon and Daniel

Lesley and I are very proud parents, Simon and Daniel have turned out to be extremely great lads, and more importantly, they love God and both are involved in the ministry in the same church where Lesley and I were the pastors. Simon is on the church leadership team as an elder and Daniel is part of the worship and creative team, they have married two lovely young ladies and produced between them three lovely grandchildren.

Simon was not a confident boy while growing up, but has matured to be someone who has gone into teaching and preaches at the church quite often. And as for Daniel, he is also a teacher, but we never expected him to become an influential leader in the church. My lads have done well, some days I stand back and look at them and thank the Lord for what I see. Being a pastor's kid is not at all plain sailing. When I make decisions in church life, sometimes they were at the end of them, but again looking back, our boys have been great. I cannot praise them highly enough in regard to their attitude, commitment and dedication to the local church.

Watching both Simon and Daniel grow, both physically

and spiritually has been heart-warming. To have my kids in church is a massive blessing, but to see them involved in the work of God is mind blowing.

My father – Irving Lakin

My dad was a coal miner, who worked down the mine at the Houghton main pit in South Yorkshire. He was a good, hard working man, who later became a Man of God. When he became a Christian, it changed our home. Although life at home was already good, it got even better. No doubt about it, he was a man who showed great faith. Such as when he and Uncle John went and bought a 53-seater bus so we could transport the children to church; and when he asked me if I would take over the leadership of the Sunday school when I was only 17 years of age. One of the things that I do not understand at all is when bad things happen to good people, to those who love God they either get sick or die. A big question for me was why did my dad had to die, at just 55 years of age? But one day when we meet again I'll find out how God used that to bring about good.

My Mother – Dorothy

My mum was a good lady who became a woman of God. Once my mother had become a Christian, she really began to love people, she began to read and believe the Bible much more and she studied to become a 'lay' preacher, so that she could go to other churches and speak. My mum just loved young people, she took charge of all the teenagers that we had in the church, and there were lots of them. She was a wonderful mentor to all of them. My mum was also very generous with her money; she would often give us money as my salary at Birmingham was low.

There was a time when Lesley and I decided to move to a new house. Whilst house hunting we heard about a detached house that looked very appealing. But when we viewed it we found it had no central heating or double glazing and a very tiny kitchen. However, we bought it. My mother then said: 'Would you like your inheritance now and not when I'm dead?' So, because of my mother's generosity we were able to put an extension on the back of the house, and put central heating and double glazing in. A Godly lady indeed. Now in heaven, enjoying life.

My Uncle - John Hunt

I really looked up to my Uncle John. Most nights after leaving work at Taylors Printers, I would call in at my Uncle John's home and stay there for about half an hour before going home; I just wanted his input into my life. He was a school teacher, but more than that he was an inspiration to me. Sadly, my Uncle John went 'home' in 2014.

Warwick Shenton

Warwick, was also once the leader of Assemblies of God (as with Paul Weaver and John Partington) he was a great man of God. I spent many hours with him and Cynthia his wife, not only when he was at camp for 12 years, but he would often come and speak at King's Christian Centre. It took me a long time to recover after he died, but he has never been forgotten. I was at his farewell service, the place was packed, standing room only. I would have loved to have worked with him, we talked about that possibility, but sadly it never happened.

Alan Hewitt

I got to know Alan better when I was part of the National Youth Council, and those ten years were really special times. Alan was the chairman of the NYC and at that time great things were happening on the youth scene. I have said before that Alan would always share part of a message that he had preached at his church and we all looked forward to hearing what he had to say. Alan is by far the best preacher I have ever heard, and I have heard quite a few preachers in my time on planet earth. There have also been times when I have asked Alan for advice on certain matters, and his wisdom was second to none.

John Partington

John and I have known each other for many years and our families have enjoyed many great holidays together. But whether on holiday or not, John is certainly good company to be with. We would laugh a lot, have great fun, do crazy things and enjoy life. For those of you who know John well, you will know that he loves to have fun. When he needs to be serious, he can be, but he just loves to enjoy life. You will never find John to be down in the dumps or depressed, as he would address the difficult things that came his way and then move on. I have been privileged to have a friend like John and Andrene, his wife, in my life. We have enjoyed many, many laughs together, and as far as the role he played as the leader of AoG, I think he has done an excellent job.

Gary Spicer

Gary and I have been friends for years, both of us play golf and at one time were both members of the same golf club. Gary is renowned for his wisdom in church life, so there were times when I needed help, and so I would go to Gary and listen to what he said. He was a massive help too in my ministry. Gary also came on board to help us with our building project, we needed his wisdom and input because it was a difficult journey. That wisdom and input were greatly appreciated. He saved us from going down the wrong path on many an occasion.

Mark Sherratt

Here is someone who knows how to live a 'balanced life', he is always the same, even if he is having a tough time in life, he would never show it. Even though he is a very busy man he will always take time out to talk, give great advice and help in any way possible, a great Man of God. Mark and I worked for a time together on the National Youth Alive Team, and it was Mark and I that organised the very first Youth Alive (National Youth Council) concert at Alton Towers. I remember going to the first meeting with those in authority and how we were 'scared' of meeting them, but God helped us and we got what we were asking for. The Alton Towers event continued for many years. Mark is not someone to blow his own trumpet even though he has built a great church in Milton Keynes.

Paul Weaver

Paul is a statesman – in what he says and does. I am very happy to call him my friend. When I worked alongside his father, there were times when I felt the pressure of being the youth pastor and working with Pastor Weaver, so on occasion I would talk to Paul on how best to solve a problem, how best to go forward after a situation and Paul would always be willing to give advice.

For 12 years Paul (along with Warwick Shenton) would come and be a speaker at one of our own youth camps. We had nine years at the Gaines Camp and three years at Blaithwaite House. Both were brilliant speakers and only heaven will reveal how many lives were touched by God during those 12 years. When I started mentoring in the Coventry church, I travelled up to Sunderland to meet up with Paul as he had written a great deal on how to mentor and this was a great help to me. Paul is part of the Minister's Golf Society and we meet up several times a year to hit a few balls!

Peter Cunningham

I got to know Peter well when he was running the Bonsall Holiday Camp in Derbyshire, and I was there to help him. We spent many years going to camp every summer, and saw God do some amazing things. Peter is a born leader and a great organiser. He comes out with a lot of dry humour and enjoys having fun. We worked extremely well together, Peter would run the business side of things and my role was to look after the kids that came to camp. It was a God sent partnership. Bonsall Camp was the place where I felt more than ever that God wanted me to work with kids. So my sincere thanks to Peter for his invaluable input into my life during all those years at Bonsall.

Mick Bonner

Mick made us very welcome at C.L.M. after we'd left King's. I found him to be a quiet man, a man of prayer and although he was the main man, he was very humble in how he conducted his life. To ask me to look into the 'health of the church' was amazing and he was not fazed by any of the reports that I presented him with. He asked me to do a few Leadership Training events with him, and his wife

Sandra would be there, offering support. He asked me to help him change how the Sunday night meetings were and to allow me once a month to preach. But the biggest thing that Mick did was to retire six months early to allow the new man the opportunity to take on the new church from day one. A gracious and amazing step to take.

Tony Williams

Tony and I have been friends for many years. When I used to take the kid's meeting at the General Conference, Tony produced all the big advertising and games boards for me. When I was the Senior Minister at King's, we employed Tony to be a Project Manager, and he worked for us for two years. He and his wife, Julie are a massive help before camp, at camp and after camp. Here is another man of

God, whenever seems to be depressed or unhappy – if sometimes he is, then he hides it well. He is a constant source of encouragement. Even when writing this book, he rings me most days to see how I am doing.

Ian Williams

Ian is part of the National Leadership team for AOG. He is a true man of God. I don't see him a lot, but when travelling somewhere he often calls to see how I am. We often share a room when playing golf and he always has some words of wisdom or encouragement for me. He is a very busy man, but he always has time for you. We have only known each other for a few years, but I am very pleased to call him my friend.

THE END

Lightning Source UK Ltd.
Milton Keynes UK
UKOW01f1835200717
305738UK00007B/455/P